New Directions for Teaching and Learning

Catherine M. Wehlburg
EDITOR-IN-CHIEF

Facilitative Collaborative Knowledge Co-Construction

Gertina J. van Schalkwyk
Rik Carl D'Amato

EDITORS

Number 143 • Fall 2015
Jossey-Bass
San Francisco

FACILITATIVE COLLABORATIVE KNOWLEDGE CO-CONSTRUCTION
Gertina J. van Schalkwyk, Rik Carl D'Amato (eds.)
New Directions for Teaching and Learning, no. 143
Catherine M. Wehlburg, Editor-in-Chief

Microfilm copies of issues and articles are available in 16 mm and 35 mm, as well as microfiche in 105 mm, through University Microfilms, Inc., 300 North Zeeb Road, Ann Arbor, MI 48106-1346.

NEW DIRECTIONS FOR TEACHING AND LEARNING (ISSN 0271-0633, electronic ISSN 1536-0768) is part of The Jossey-Bass Higher and Adult Education Series and is published quarterly by Wiley Subscription Services, Inc., A Wiley Company, at Jossey-Bass, One Montgomery Street, Suite 1200, San Francisco, CA 94104-4594. POSTMASTER: Send address changes to New Directions for Teaching and Learning, Jossey-Bass, One Montgomery Street, Suite 1200, San Francisco, CA 94104-4594.

New Directions for Teaching and Learning is indexed in CIJE: Current Index to Journals in Education (ERIC), Contents Pages in Education (T&F), Educational Research Abstracts Online (T&F), ERIC Database (Education Resources Information Center), Higher Education Abstracts (Claremont Graduate University), and SCOPUS (Elsevier).

INDIVIDUAL SUBSCRIPTION RATE (in USD): $89 per year US/Can/Mex, $113 rest of world; institutional subscription rate: $335 US, $375 Can/Mex, $409 rest of world. Single copy rate: $29. Electronic only–all regions: $89 individual, $335 institutional; Print & Electronic–US: $98 individual, $402 institutional; Print & Electronic–Can/Mex: $98 individual, $442 institutional; Print & Electronic–rest of world: $122 individual, $476 institutional.

Cover design: Wiley
Cover Images: © Lava 4 images | Shutterstock

EDITORIAL CORRESPONDENCE should be sent to the editor-in-chief, Catherine M. Wehlburg, c.wehlburg@tcu.edu.

www.josseybass.com

CONTENTS

FROM THE SERIES EDITOR

About This Publication

Since 1980, *New Directions for Teaching and Learning* (NDTL) has brought a unique blend of theory, research, and practice to leaders in postsecondary education. NDTL sourcebooks strive not only for solid substance but also for timeliness, compactness, and accessibility.

The series has four goals: to inform readers about current and future directions in teaching and learning in postsecondary education, to illuminate the context that shapes these new directions, to illustrate these new direction through examples from real settings, and to propose ways in which these new directions can be incorporated into still other settings.

This publication reflects the view that teaching deserves respect as a high form of scholarship. We believe that significant scholarship is conducted not only by researchers who report results of empirical investigations but also by practitioners who share disciplinary reflections about teaching. Contributors to NDTL approach questions of teaching and learning as seriously as they approach substantive questions in their own disciplines, and they deal not only with pedagogical issues but also with the intellectual and social context in which these issues arise. Authors deal on the one hand with theory and research and on the other with practice, and they translate from research and theory to practice and back again.

About This Volume

The purpose of this second volume of a two-part series is to build on the foundation that was laid in *New Directions for Teaching and Learning* #142. In that first volume, the authors provided a framework that was designed to encourage teachers as they move from a Confucian way of teaching toward a more collaborative way of providing a co-constructed knowledge base in the classroom. There has been a great deal of research and practice focusing on collaborative learning and the positive relationships that are developed among students and educators when knowledge is viewed as something that is constructed together. This volume acknowledges the research provided by fields such as neuropsychology and the application to teaching. While the focus is specifically on Asian students, the information in this volume can be used for all students and educators who are engaged in the collaborative search for knowledge.

Catherine M. Wehlburg
Editor-in-Chief

PROLOGUE

Dedications

To the many students I have taught at the University of Macau and with whom I have collaborated in the co-construction of knowledge, I dedicate this book and wish you all the best for success and well-being in your careers and in life!
—Gertina J. van Schalkwyk
To the people of China and the billions and billions of Asian people who have so much to say to the world. I dedicate this book to you and wish you health, freedom, and prosperity as you change our world. I hope we listen and work with you.
—Rik Carl D'Amato

Prologue

Choreographing a collaborative teaching and learning environment aims to facilitate the internalization of skills and attitudes where students can appreciate their personal knowledge as much as that provided in textbooks, and where students can develop confidence in their learning and personalized knowledge. The students engage in different dances among themselves and with the instructor as they collaboratively reflect upon existing knowledge systems, explore different perspectives, and move, for example, from just learning and memorizing theoretical constructs to thinking about the influence of personal experiences, and to interpreting observations in accordance with relevant theories or empirical work.

The shift toward outcomes-based collaborative teaching and learning in Asian higher education settings poses multiple challenges to both the instructor and the student. When combining these challenges with teaching a complex subject matter, one is further faced with finding ways to design, plan, and arrange the sequence of learning activities in such a way that the Asian student will be motivated to engage fully with the subject matter in a practical and applied manner, and to create knowledge that resonates not only for a future career but also in her or his personal life. Students need to develop a critical awareness of theoretical knowledge and integrate their own "expert knowledge" through relational practice, thus moving away from passive learning to a position of negotiating alternatives through constructive conflict. Both instructor and students should become reflective improvisers on the learning stage and in the co-construction of new ideas, thoughts, and meanings.

It may be challenging to choreograph and facilitate the processes that unfold on the collaborative teaching and learning stage. It is also quite rewarding in the sense that students in Asia, despite their initial reluctance to communicate in a second language, become active participants in the co-construction of new knowledge and finding solutions to problems. In collaboration with the instructor, with one another, and with the subject matter, the students' local knowledge and experiences are challenged and they come to recognize the place of personal reflection in the process of co-constructing new meanings. Thus, choreographing teaching and learning in a facilitative and collaborative way makes it a valuable opportunity for creating a coherent knowledge framework in Asian higher education settings. Instead of the fragmentation that is often the result when learning units are kept separate and the subject matter is taught in an input-driven style, the knowledge, skills, and attitudes acquired through a collaborative teaching and learning approach become a way of life with influence across a wide spectrum of settings.

The chapters in this volume aim to elaborate on the rhetoric in Part 1, *From the Confucian Way to Collaborative Knowledge Co-Construction*, providing further foundational frameworks that underlie the move toward a facilitative and collaborative way of knowledge construction. In Part 2, *Facilitative Collaborative Knowledge Co-Construction*, the author of Chapter 1 reviews the major paradigm shift in education toward constructivist learning and the lessons learned in facilitating cooperative and collaborative learning. As collaborative teaching and learning are firmly entrenched in developing positive relationships and the processes of social construction, the authors of Chapter 2 explore the importance of relational intelligence and cooperative action, also providing a practical example of implementing these strategies in collaborative teaching and learning. Facilitative and collaborative teaching and learning should also acknowledge the valuable insights provided by neuropsychology and the useful information that can be gained from appropriate diagnostics to ensure that Asian students can benefit from the learning experience in higher education (Chapter 3). Collaborative teaching and learning should also facilitate sociocognitive skills and emotional intelligence to assist the students in making connections between the brain functions and their own emotions during the processes of learning and co-constructing new meanings (Chapter 4). Promoting the nurturing processes that will encourage students to optimize their performance on the learning stage, the final chapter provides some practical hints for engendering critical reflective thinking within a collaborative teaching and learning context.

One can certainly train students to memorize facts and follow algorithms, but unless they know what the algorithms mean and when and how to use them, their mastery of the subject is only superficial. Moreover, most of the knowledge that is acquired by rote learning will be lost quickly because it has no connection to anything meaningful in the students' minds and lives. We view the Asian student and every other student as meaning-generating performers on the learning stage and instructors in higher education as choreographers of the desired outcomes. People create understanding and knowledge with each other through collaborative actions. Outcomes-based collaborative teaching and learning enhance teaching excellence in Asian higher education, and promote knowledge co-construction that is interesting, relevant, and worth pursuing in the world of work and as a lifelong performance goal.

Gertina J. van Schalkwyk
Rik Carl D'Amato
Editors

GERTINA J. VAN SCHALKWYK is an associate professor of psychology in the Department of Psychology, and former coordinator for professional development in the Centre for Teaching and Learning Enhancement at the University of Macau, China.

RIK CARL D'AMATO is a professor of psychology on the faculty of the Chicago School for Professional Psychology, and former director of the Centre for Teaching and Learning Enhancement at the University of Macau, China.

NEW DIRECTIONS FOR TEACHING AND LEARNING • DOI: 10.1002/tl

1

This chapter explores the move toward a constructivist paradigm and collaborative knowledge construction in the broader institutional context of education.

Knowledge Construction: A Paradigm Shift

Hugh Gash

In the past generation, significant changes have taken place in educational thinking in many countries. These changes are due to advances in the psychology of learning. More recently these theoretical advances are being implemented in the ways we teach. This chapter focuses on some of these changes and their theoretical and social context. The purpose of the chapter is specifically to examine research in collaborative knowledge construction with a view to presenting this perspective on education in terms of its origins and its implementation with an emphasis on teacher education. The broader aim is to stimulate thinking about novel ways of working with students in contemporary universities with a focus on their personal development in the digital age. Developments in this area are considered from a constructivist perspective, as advances in this educational approach are beginning to be more broadly understood as providing a framework supporting educational achievement in a socially responsible context (Tobias and Duffy 2009).

The chapter begins with an introduction to constructivist theory as it applies to educational practice. Collaborative knowledge construction needs to consider education from three interrelated points of view: how the individual learner builds knowledge, how this construction may be facilitated by collaborative learning using interaction with peers, and the broader institutional context of the education process supporting measures needed to develop these new ways of working with students and maintaining these approaches with staff collaboration and support. The approach taken here allows examination of the values implicit in different forms of educational tradition, and considers data from international comparison data on student achievement, especially as these data apply to a number of Asian educational systems (OECD 2011; TIMSS 1995, 2007).

Furthermore, the chapter makes a number of assumptions about educational processes. The first is that ways of facilitating learning for groups of students at one age level are likely to be important for groups at other

New Directions for Teaching and Learning, no. 143, Fall 2015 © 2015 Wiley Periodicals, Inc.
Published online in Wiley Online Library (wileyonlinelibrary.com) • DOI: 10.1002/tl.20133

levels. On this basis, ideas coming from research on group learning at different levels across the educational spectrum can enrich the aims of this chapter. A second assumption is that the procedures used to facilitate collaborative learning in any curriculum area will be of interest and relevant to considering how to initiate similar procedures in other curriculum areas. The collaborative learning research projects reviewed focused on mathematics teaching and learning, and literacy. The main themes, however, in such projects have to do with ways of facilitating the instructor's professional identity so that the students become more engaged in their learning and learn how to work together in a productive way.

A Recent Historical Perspective

The 1960s were a time of cultural and educational change, and in 1968 students rioted in many countries, including the United States, France, and Japan (Kreis 2009). The educational changes were characterized by a move from traditional teacher-directed forms of pedagogy to more learner-centered approaches. The traditional approaches were principally concerned with transmitting information, and the learners' success in education depended heavily on memorizing the taught curriculum. In the educational sphere in the British Isles, the Plowden Report (1967) signaled this change from teacher-directed educational strategies to more child-centered approaches at the primary educational level. Shortly afterward in Ireland a new curriculum (Ireland 1971) was published. These moves away from the traditional model were based on forms of constructivist theory and were concerned with primary education. Their success was hampered by variations in the way constructivist approaches were interpreted.

The variations in understandings of constructivism are entirely consistent with the idea that we construct our understandings through our encounters with others and our experience. All constructivist approaches emphasize the importance of the role of the constructor in assembling knowledge, but there are variations in the emphasis put on the role of instructors in the process of constructing knowledge. A contentious constructivist idea is that cognitively we are limited by our experiences and cannot go outside them. While this is an important idea for educators who are concerned with actively researching students and pupils, it is often taken to threaten the status quo as it is interpreted as implying that anything goes (Larochelle and Désautels 2011).

Key issues for all educational practice are the aims or objectives that instructors have in mind when they teach and the procedures they put in place to achieve these aims. There are also tensions between the short-term academic need to do well in exams and the longer-term social need to educate young people so that they will be well equipped to work collaboratively with their peers and become lifelong learners. Indeed, this challenge is the underlying theme of the present chapter. Schools are particularly vulnerable to pressure from parents and school management to ensure that their students perform well in final examinations. A challenge today for educators is to provide broad educational experiences in schools and universities so that knowledge is learned effectively in ways that facilitate productive participation in society following formal schooling and education. More generally, in the twenty-first century the challenge is to provide educational experiences that fit with the students' potential future life experiences.

Constructivist Learning.   I want to outline some key issues in this movement as they have a bearing on the exciting changes and opportunities that are the topic of this chapter. The central issue has to do with a new way of thinking about education. A key feature of this way of thinking requires more flexibility in our traditional approaches to education and in particular about teaching and learning. Language invites people to think of teaching as an activity for teachers and of learning as another activity for learners. I think one reason it has been difficult for educational systems to adapt is because teaching and learning are so fundamental and seemingly beyond change, though the use of the phrase *teaching-learning* is a sign that the two activities are dynamically related at the interface between teachers and learners.

One change promoted by the curriculum developments in Ireland and England in the 1960s was a shift in focus from the teacher as teacher of a set curriculum to an emphasis on the learner as a problem solver. This implied a shift in the role of the teacher from giving information to the learner to a role of partnership between teacher and learner, with the teacher as a partner facilitating the emergence of novel ways of understanding in the learner. Traditionally, direct teaching has its methods of presenting set material in interesting ways and then ensuring that the students know what was taught with an emphasis on memory. This method minimizes student differences and may assume that students will have little difficulty learning the material or they are all learning at the same speed. Difficulties arise quickly when some students show different aptitudes for the material. In this case, either the ones who learn quickly have to wait or the ones who learn more slowly are left behind and the danger is that many will cease to engage with learning. More student-centered approaches engage all students in educationally related tasks so that the tasks they are working on provide opportunities to learn. To facilitate this, the material may be presented through cooperative activity.

A second change has to do with the views taken of the curriculum, and there are a number of perspectives. Teachers are frequently under pressure to consider the curriculum as content or knowledge to be transmitted, and there are variations in the preferred approach taken (ranging from promoting individual student rote learning to setting up various forms of student problem solving). Traditionally, there has been a widespread tendency to hold on to the desire to facilitate the learning of set pieces of competence. Children must learn to read, to write, and to analyze different domains of knowledge in set ways. Secondary (high) schools in particular are insistent on this because in many countries they are concerned with students knowing set content to help them pass university entrance examinations. I suspect that other countries are like Ireland, where it has been hard to find examples of student-centered learning in secondary schools. My own view is that there are undoubtedly pockets of excellent constructivist practice at all levels.

A study, which was mainly about mathematics teaching in the secondary school program, demonstrates forcibly the prevalence of didactic teaching. Lyons and her colleagues (2003) studied pupils and teachers in secondary schools in Ireland to examine the practices surrounding the preparation for a national examination held when pupils are about 15 years of age. Their results revealed the prevalence of drill and practice and a strong didactic approach as the norm for the teachers who participated. The teachers tended to see learning as principally about memorizing formulas and procedures rather than teaching to provide reasons for solutions, or teaching to think creatively. Significantly, the pattern was similar for the teaching of English, where 92 percent of the classroom discourse was teacher-directed, though there was scope for more interpretation from the pupils. The power relationship where the teacher was the expert and the pupil was to listen and remember characterized both English teaching and mathematics teaching.

A contrast can be made in comparing traditional teacher-focused learning with newer approaches in terms of where the learning is located and whether the emphasis is on the process of learning or the product to be learned. Underlying these variations in ideas about the curriculum is a rather difficult shift in ways we can think about knowing and knowledge. For many, these changes were based on ways of thinking reflected by John Dewey and Jean Piaget that recognized the importance of children's activity in learning. This view presented learning as the result of purposive activity designed to reduce uncertainty and to create ways of understanding regularities noticed in experience. Emergence of such knowledge is often facilitated in class through group work or discussion, and it requires new skills from teachers—often very different skills than the teachers know implicitly from their own experiences of schooling. This lack, I think, is why it is often difficult to promote constructive collaborative learning models in schools. If this process of collaborative constructive learning works, it is because insightful instructors have the capacity and desire to think about the various dynamic balances involved in the learners' thinking. The students are balancing past experiences with the ongoing experiences in the classroom. Some of these relate to the class content, which may or may not be engaging, and others relate to interpersonal relations between the instructor and the other students. The instructor is trying to organize the students' experiences in the classroom so that they will engage with the topic and find it absorbing in ways that ensure they learn and participate effectively in the learning community.

Constructivist Theory.   In constructivist theory, the human cognitive system notices differences and operates to resolve them. Such noticing requires items to notice, and the items themselves may be emerging and changing. Piaget's (1970) theory is an example of a constructivist epistemology. In his theory the process of acquiring knowledge is called equilibration, emphasizing the need to maintain a balance between what was understood and what is emerging in ongoing experience. A key idea is that the conditions for knowledge creation occur when the learner notices a mismatch between elements in experience and features of knowledge already learned. A mismatch or noticed difference provides a challenge to the cognitive system. Suitable optimum challenges motivate the learner who will be empowered by solving the problem. If the challenge is too easy, the learner will become bored, and if it is too hard, the learner may become discouraged. The learner balances previous knowledge and ongoing experience at two levels. The learner must initially balance personal intra-individual ideas with social inter-individual ideas. The need to understand regularities in experience is constrained by these intra-individual and inter-individual balances. The new insights have to be invented in this context, so "to understand is to invent," as Piaget (1973) put it in the title of one of his books. The task of the instructor who desires implementing classroom activities based on a constructivist model like this is to design experiences for the learner that will facilitate the invention of new understandings and the mapping of new knowledge. In fact, learning that does not permit this type of meaning making is dismissed as trivial learning because it is unlikely to last (von Foerster 2003). In other approaches, one would say that what is learned is unlikely to move from short-term memory to long-term memory.

Constructivist ideas about learning have posed a direct challenge to more traditional educational ideas. The emphasis on the intrapersonal in this theory of learning led many instructors to emphasize the importance of play and discovery learning in the classroom. Nonconstructivist educators have criticized constructivist approaches to learning because of the time wasted while children explore tasks that they may not be ready to learn (Tobias and Duffy 2009). An extensive debate took place on this topic at the American Educational Research Conference in 2007. These discussions were wide-ranging and important for understanding constructivist instruction, but here two variables concern us: (1) whether the educational issues were best assessed using achievement scores, and (2) the role of the instructor. On the latter issue, it is clear that there was a meeting of the opposing views and constructivist instructors are recognized to have an important role in designing constructivist learning environments for students and in guiding them during their learning, but it is not the traditional role of imparting information (Tobias and Duffy 2009).

In the debates between radical constructivism and social constructionism, the importance of the intrapersonal moment of learning is called into
question. Von Glasersfeld (1987) applied the term *radical constructivism* to
Piaget's theory and to educational settings for a variety of reasons, mainly
to highlight that we cannot match our experience with reality. We always
interpret in terms of what we know. So instructors have to develop a profound understanding of what is commonplace but difficult to keep sight of
in class—namely that students interpret what the instructor says according
to each student's cognitive organization and not according to the carefully
constructed message the instructor presents. Certainly, the student's social
experience is critical, but students always interpret instructors' messages
using prior knowledge. Consequently, learning is most likely to occur in
collaborative work with others, where there are increased opportunities for
students' existing knowledge to be challenged and so for cognitive change
to occur. This shift in emphasis requires a reorganization of the instructors'
priorities. Important consequences are the types of teaching and work that
this chapter is concerned with, hence the notion of a paradigm shift.

The paradigm shift is necessary for a variety of reasons. One is because
if this constructivist model of communication is taken seriously we need to
change our practices in education; another is that in this twenty-first century it is evident that knowledge is available in so many ways, including the
web, that the idea that learning is dependent on one expert imparting information in traditional ways is outdated. An implication of the constructivist
epistemology is that not only are there different ways of thinking about
experience, but there are also alternative ways of doing things, each with
its own advantages and constraints. Not all of them are viable, of course,
but people make choices and live with the consequences. I wonder if the
ongoing debates about constructivist education are not due to increasing
awareness of multiple points of view in our lives, and some find this more
positive than others. Importantly, too, the paradigm shift implicit in the
constructivist model has deep ethical implications.

Changes in the relationship between instructor and student and learning that depend on constructivist understandings of how thinking works
have implications at different levels of the educational process. The previous sections have emphasized changes in the teaching-learning relationship, and implicit in these changes are other fundamental changes in the
relationship between instructor, student, and knowledge. If learning is prioritized more as it is in student-centered approaches, then the balance of
initiative changes. The students' role is necessarily more active and more
critical, whereas in previous times the teachers' role was more active and
the students' role was more compliant and passive. The traditional educational model required students to know set pieces of knowledge, and failure
to remember was assessed by the mismatch with the set pieces. One could
be wrong in clearly specified ways. Knowledge was power, and the product
was static. In a changing world where the ability to cope with change is

important and where what is important are the processes of investigation and ways of finding solutions, then alternative ways of finding solutions become more important than knowing what worked in the past. In such an educational system, the ability of the partners in learning to collaborate and work as a team is an important feature of the process of finding solutions that work. Now what is important is that the process is working for a viable solution, and power is not located in conformity to what did work in the past but what will work now (and in the future). In a society that is rapidly changing, ways of thinking about the educational process that include in the model creative, active students become more and more important.

While I do not pretend to provide an exhaustive coverage of the research in this area, I am confident that the descriptions offered of the research reviewed will give readers insights into the importance of new developments, inviting and encouraging them to seriously consider new ways of designing learning environments for their own practices.

Asian Success in Educational Rankings

The next section is devoted to a brief analysis of the differences between some Asian countries and other countries in terms of educational achievement. This provides important context because there have been some spectacular successes in a number of Asian countries and in advising how to implement the constructive collaborative learning model it is important to understand how this paradigm change fits with current best practice and why it should be applied.

The Third International Maths and Science Study (TIMSS) with fourth- and eighth-grade students (TIMSS 1995) and the Organization for Economic Cooperation and Development's (OECD) Program for International Student Assessment (PISA) with 15-year-old students (OECD 2011) allow comparisons of different educational systems at an international level. In addition, there is considerable research establishing models best practices in national school systems, and I believe that advances made can be used to consider how to promote collaborative teaching and learning in the university sector. TIMSS (2007) and PISA (OECD 2011) evidence are based on national comparisons of samples of primary and secondary school pupils. The achievement measures provide a platform to examine educational practice in high- and low-achieving countries. Of course, these differences must be understood in the context of the tensions just referred to between achievement scores and the ability to work together in socially productive ways. In addition, there are differences in the preferred or optimum ways to do this research.

The final issue of the American Educational Research Association's sponsored journal *Educational Researcher* in 2008 was devoted to an analysis of the American National Mathematics Advisory Panel Final Report. That report included only evaluations of mathematics programs that used experimental design studies with control groups. A number of the authors in the *Educational Researcher* (Kelly 2008) took issue with this research design restriction. They argued that knowledge about best practice in mathematics teaching was not wholly the preserve of such studies, and ignored important insights into best practice in mathematics teaching by narrowing the sample of research reviewed in this way.

The striking message of these international comparison studies is of the excellence of the academic achievement in a number of Asian countries. Japan, Singapore, Hong Kong, and South Korea were at the top of those countries sampled in their academic achievement (TIMSS 2007). There was slight variation between these countries depending on whether the studies were referring to mathematics or science and to 9-year-olds or 13-year-olds, but the point is that these countries are performing at the highest levels in comparison with other countries in the world. This trend of Asian excellence continues in the more recent TIMSS (2007) studies, and Taiwanese students have joined the ranks of the highest achievers. The OECD international assessment of 15-year-olds also shows very high Asian achievement for the pupils studied in Mainland China, South Korea, Hong Kong, and Singapore (OECD 2011).

Educational comparisons are useful tools to begin to question schools' effectiveness. In understanding the meaning of these tests, one needs to know details about how the test was constructed and what types of items were used. In the case of the TIMSS (2007) study, there have been analyses of the questions on the tests. In the context of the present chapter, one interesting analysis has to do with the extent that the test assesses problem-solving capability. This ability is important from the constructivist perspective, as it is less a matter of reproducing material presented in class and more a matter of being process oriented and of reflecting about the test problems. As we shall see later in the chapter, mathematical problem solving was made a priority in the education of pupils in Singapore 19 years ago, and Singapore is one of the high-scoring Asian countries in these international comparison studies (Kaur, Har, and Kapur 2009). Samples of items used in the current version of TIMSS are available on the web. One such sample for science questions for fourth- and eighth-grade students is provided through the Irish Educational Research Centre (www.erc.ie/?p=169). Dossey, O'Sullivan, and Gonzales (2006) published an analysis of the items in terms of their capacity to measure problem solving. This analysis gives insight into the ways the test developers have sought to move beyond knowing that to knowing how—that is, from product to process. In the case of the TIMSS items, for example, knowing facts and procedures in TIMSS corresponds to reproduction in PISA, and reasoning in TIMSS corresponds to reflection in PISA.

While it is reassuring to know that the capacity to reason is being assessed in addition to knowing facts, a critical skill for education is for learners to know how to learn in a collaborative sense with their peers. People vary in their capacity to work with others, but if the skills to do this are imparted largely in the home and not in school, many will not reach their full potential. Successful economies need innovative teams in today's world. Earlier, I mentioned the contrast between constructivist education and more direct instruction via guided worked examples. These examples have a role in science teaching, but learners also need to be able to engage in activities such as modeling, arguing, and evaluating in order to assess knowledge claims and restructure knowledge via conceptual change. Classes in Singapore, for example, are quite crowded and there is heavy demand for classroom teaching and nonteaching duties requiring strong instructor-centered control, especially in large classes, and there is only about 8.5 percent group work (Wong et al. 2009). Nonetheless, there are advantages to seeking ways to augment the amount of cooperative work for the benefit of the students in the world of work—even when working with large classes. The following section places this need for collaborative work in the context of constructivist learning approaches, taking account of the need to attend to the different levels of learning—the individual, the interpersonal, and the macro school system levels.

Moving to a Constructivist Perspective

Often education is broadly conceived as a preparation for society. In Ireland (Ireland 1999, 7), for example, the general aims of education are: (1) to enable the child to live a full life as a child, (2) to realize his or her potential as a unique individual, (3) to enable the child to develop as a social being through living and cooperating with others and so contribute to the good of society, and (4) to prepare the child for further education and lifelong learning. While these aims were part of the Irish Primary Curriculum, they relate closely to the broad aims of the OECD for the knowledge economy: There are additional "workplace competencies" needed in the knowledge economy. Communication skills, problem-solving skills, the ability to work in teams, and information and communications technology (ICT) skills, among others, are becoming important and complementary to basic core or foundation skills. Even more than other workers, knowledge workers rely on workplace competencies.

Consequently, when analyzing international comparisons, educators should take care to see that not only do the educational approaches used provide excellent opportunities for pupils and students to learn but also that this is done in a way that contributes to society. In trying to make sense of national differences reported in TIMSS (1995) and PISA (OECD 2011), a variety of other factors are relevant. For example, the educational expertise of instructors tends to be higher in higher-scoring countries, and the tendency for instructors to work collaboratively together planning and evaluating lessons occurs frequently in countries that achieve higher scores in national comparisons between East Asian countries and the United States

(Wang and Lin 2005). An analysis of educational data for the United States and China suggests that there is not sufficient evidence to show a positive relationship between the implementation of curriculum standards, class organization, instructors' mathematics knowledge, teaching practice, and high mathematics performance by students. It may be that the difference between Chinese and US students in mathematics achievement is due to language features or other nonschool factors like student self-concept or family values (Wang and Lin 2005). Also, it may be that the collaborative learning opportunities for the instructors concerned are playing a critical role.

So how could one account for the success of the various Asian countries in these international comparison studies? This is a key issue, and there are some clues that I present with reference to the constructivist learning model outlined earlier. However, there is likely to be no one simple answer, so other recent developments in the domain of collaborative learning are also presented to provide insight into models of recent ways of organizing these types of learning.

Lesson Study. A promising first element in this analysis is the examination of the highly collaborative method used in Japan called *lesson study*. One of the key ideas in lesson study is the examination of lessons that work and the collaboration of groups of instructors concentrating on, for example, mathematics problems that cause difficulties for students so that instructors can develop lessons that work better (Cerbin and Kopp 2006). Practically all Japanese instructors use this model during any school year, and it was adapted for use by Cerbin and Kopp initially in their own university in Wisconsin to help improve staff teaching. The aim is to use lesson plans and analyze their use so that detailed lesson plans are available together with research on how the plans worked to enable student learning. These plans are presented in sufficient detail so that this research can be replicated. Over a three-year period, the approach was found to be so successful that it was extended to 10 different campuses across the University of Wisconsin system, including 25 different disciplines. So the model is a flexible model that works for faculty professional development in teaching and learning.

The working of the lesson plan model is suited to facilitating constructivist approaches for a number of reasons. First, instructors work together in small groups, so they have an opportunity to reflect on their own ideas and ways of teaching that are likely to lead to new understandings. Second, the discussions that take place among the instructors prioritize a type of cognitive empathy with the students in terms of how students are likely to think about the topic, what prior knowledge they have, and what sorts of issues lead to misconceptions. In a constructivist framework a key part of teaching is to find ways to present information to students that will be at an appropriate level for the students to change their own ways of thinking, as information that is too complex will perhaps be remembered in the short term but not integrated easily into the students' own ways of thinking.

NEW DIRECTIONS FOR TEACHING AND LEARNING • DOI: 10.1002/tl

These factors will have an influence on how best to present the topic to the students while the instructors benefit from one another's insights into the topic and how to resolve these issues together. Providing a context to discuss student preconceptions and the most effective ways to facilitate their interpretation of the topic is a novel opportunity for many college instructors to reflect on their teaching. It also provides them an opportunity to work on a lesson-by-lesson basis to improve their teaching in a systematic and reflective way.

Small Group Instruction.   In a constructivist learning environment, teachers guide students' learning so that they have opportunities to reconsider the emerging ideas they have about a topic. Collaborative student learning offers opportunities to reconsider ideas in discussion and facilitates the development of social skills. Good, Mulryan, and McCaslin (1992) discussed small group work in relation to the following characteristics: active learning, opportunities for peer interaction, enhanced opportunity for mathematical thinking, instructor as curriculum developer, implementing new tasks, assigning student roles, student passivity, and accountability. Many of these elements relate to the design of constructivist learning opportunities. In particular, issues relating to curriculum deserve some comment because textbooks favor individual rather than group work. In their review, instructors were often left to their own creativity in developing suitable tasks for the students (Good, Mulryan, and McCaslin 1992). This is not the case in approaches using lesson study, although care is needed that the lesson study approach is not a substitute for textbook material.

Dwyer (2010) examined classroom behaviors as students and instructors learned to use online resources effectively in groups. This required a balance between instructor intervention and student involvement in collaborative learning. The digital resources were used for reading lessons, science, and social studies. Students were observed during their learning experiences and also interviewed. Dwyer showed that the role of the instructor changed over time, with scaffolding decreasing and students' increasingly taking responsibility. As the year progressed, instructors became facilitators and colearners, and students increasingly relied on one another as partners.

Data analysis showed that patterns of student behavior emerged during the year facilitating peer collaboration and leading to the social construction of knowledge in groups. There were four themes: peers supported each other in their groups, they asked questions that led to differentiation of ideas, they helped each other to be more efficient in their work, and they developed ways of discussing tasks that included showing as well as talking, as words can sometimes obscure meaning. Teachers assigned specific roles to the group members. These included questioner, navigator, and summarizer. The navigator's job included assessing the reliability of information; for example, a governmental site might be more reliable than a commercial one, and the navigators were encouraged to detect errors. Group work also allowed the participants to ask questions to expand their own ideas and evaluate them together. Being on task included planning, questioning, and evaluating progress (Dwyer 2010). Butler and Gash (2003) had shown previously that such collaborative self-regulation helped self-confidence.

Student Cooperative Learning.   Corcoran (2008) studied collaborative learning among student instructors planning cooperatively to teach mathematics in Irish primary schools using the lesson study method. Success in mathematics in Irish secondary schools traditionally depends on memorization of formulas and procedures. As instructors are likely to begin teaching using techniques they experienced as students, it was hoped that the opportunity to work together collaboratively preparing these lessons would provide a model for the instructors to help their pupils to learn collaboratively. The Irish Primary Curriculum is explicitly constructivist, but a reliance on textbooks in various subjects, including mathematics, contradicts its spirit.

Initially Corcoran (2008) gave the student instructors a mathematics ability test. She then observed a small group of participating students teaching, and finally she arranged for small groups of students to work together collaboratively in a lesson study exercise to plan their mathematics lessons for teaching in primary schools. The key dimensions of classroom teaching that she focused on were specified in the Rowland, Huckstep, and Thwaites (2005) knowledge quartet: foundation, transformation, connection, and contingency. While Corcoran was concerned with constructivist mathematics teaching and learning, the processes she described are germane for pedagogical practices in other domains of knowledge. Foundation is the basic understanding of the subject matter. Transformation is about the instructors' ability to change the information so that it's accessible to students, for example, by choice of suitable examples. Connection is about meaningful lesson sequencing, and contingency is the capacity to deviate from the plan—to cope with the unexpected.

These four categories provide significant and interesting insights into the students' actual teaching. Corcoran (2008) undertook this assessment in the context of her doctoral thesis. A staff development initiative at the university level could use similar procedures with, for example, video recordings of lectures. Possibly the knowledge quartet categories used would change in response to needs that may vary the teaching-learning environment in classes at the tertiary level. However, the following gives a more precise idea of insights into the teaching process gained from the four categories described.

In the analysis of the students' teaching, in some cases the children were clearly working on problems that were based on textbooks but were not socially relevant to them (Corcoran 2008; Dooley 2010). So the work probably did not facilitate meaning making as recommended by constructivist practice. Some student instructors taught by questioning, prompting, and encouraging children to reason about the material, and others talked to the pupils. Some student instructors provided more structure to the lessons but others were more concerned with the actual working experience in groups. Overall, student instructors used different organizational strategies: some were very clear but constrained by the topic and less concerned with the activities that the class was engaged in, whereas others in contrast provided engaging group activities and were less concerned with presentation of set materials. A critical issue is whether recall or understanding is prioritized, and reflection on the activities is needed to promote the type of constructivist teaching presented in the curriculum.

After observing student instructors teaching, the next step to facilitate constructivist practice with these students was to implement the lesson study approach collaboratively (Cerbin and Kopp 2006; Fang, Lee, and Sharifah-Thalha 2009). The students prepared lessons to teach in primary schools. By watching videos of these lessons being taught, the students became aware of their mathematical strengths and weaknesses and of the need to connect the content to the pupils' other experiences of the material. This was the first time the student instructors had an opportunity for others to observe their work. As the lesson study process continued, engagement improved substantially and the students spent more and more time preparing the activities and discovering how to teach mathematics well. The researcher's role changed as the group learned to control itself.

As the student instructors worked collaboratively, their engagement, their alignment with their colleagues, and their participation in this community of practice created a new group identity. They discovered that lesson study was a way to stop teaching as they had been taught. Preparing lessons, delivering them, and then reflecting on them in a group enabled change and helped them to be more comfortable with their uncertainties about teaching. Group collaboration became an accessible form of professional development (Cerbin and Kopp 2006; Fang, Lee, and Sharifah-Thalha 2009).

Finally, Corcoran (2008) considered introducing this type of approach in schools. Some instructors feel it would be hard to put in place, but it has worked in England. As a model of educational practice, it would require support at both school level and school system level. The next section will return to this issue.

The Importance of Learner Uncertainty

Corcoran (2008) provided a model of cooperative learning at the tertiary level for use with students. Dooley (2010), on the other hand, illustrated how lecturers and instructors can facilitate the emergence of new ideas by looking at conversations in class, focusing on moments of pupil uncertainty in learning. Initially Dooley specified the constructs that she hoped the pupils would learn by engaging with the class materials. What is important here is the construction of new ideas by students, and this is a special moment that requires instructor sensitivity. Dooley identified three aspects of this process for instructors: epistemic actions, hedges and pronouns, and follow-up moves.

The learner epistemic actions were recognizing, building, and constructing (Hershkowitz, Schwartz, and Dreyfus 2001). Hedges and pronouns were signals that learners were puzzled. They used pronouns like "it" to refer to symbols like square roots, indicating they had an uncertain idea that was part of an emerging meaning structure. Saying "maybe," "I think," or "possibly" was an indication pupils were wondering how to organize intuitive impressions to allow ideas to emerge (Rowland 1992, 1995).

For the instructor, the art is to develop a set of procedures fostering conjectural ideas so that students are not afraid to be wrong and are encouraged to work with their uncertainties. The instructor follow-up moves were promptings, scaffoldings, and supports that instructors can give to students to allow emergence of uncertain ideas. Such "almost there" ideas are ones that seem important to the instructor but the learner may not recognize this. Instructor follow-up moves include adding to a learner's contribution (e.g., elaborating, suggesting, correcting), eliciting something from a learner (e.g., who has a good idea that needs to be drawn out), pressing or encouraging the learner to say more about a tentative idea, maintaining (asking the learner to continue or to repeat), and confirming an idea the instructor heard. Indeed, Dooley admitted she was initially uncomfortable repeating statements made by students as she considered this bad educational practice, but later she recognized that "revoicing" supported student intuitions so that newly constructed ideas could emerge. She referred to a "conjectural attitude" as critical in such teaching. This is the nurturing of uncertainty allowing the emergence of new ideas (Mason 2008). Conjectural thought allowed these ideas into the public domain where they could be sifted to see what worked and was valuable.

Dooley (2010) found that constructed insights were often associated with the other two epistemic actions of recognizing and building in the lessons she examined. In some productive lessons, the group shared these actions. When the group had a common purpose, it seemed that more group members took on supportive functions for the emergence of new constructions. Often pupils in pairs or small groups constructed ideas that fed into the plenary discussion at the end of class. So the extended whole-class discussion could be a powerful vehicle for consolidating insights. Recently, the importance of constructivist educational practices has been debated in relation to mathematics education (Tobias and Duffy 2009). This debate contrasts the importance of direct instruction with the values and benefits of constructivist approaches (Gash 2009). Gresalfi and Lester (2009) robustly made the case for the social benefits of the constructivist approach, emphasizing the importance of participating in particular practices in a social activity system.

Facilitating Constructivist Instructor Development

Eithne Kennedy (2010) completed a landmark study on instructor professional development designed to improve poor reading standards in a disadvantaged school in Dublin. The study received an outstanding dissertation award in 2010 from the International Reading Association. In moving from mathematics teaching to reading, it broadens the discussion here and focuses on key features in instructor development. It aimed to boost literacy achievement by engaging the children in reading and writing.

Kennedy (2010) worked with instructors in a school effectively forming a collaborative instructor network. Like other research reported here, it stressed the importance of the whole school approach, of collaboration with external partners who model good practice, and of being grounded in the content of teaching. Also, it emphasized constructivist teaching principles and aimed to improve student achievement. Instructors in the study attended workshops on teaching reading. They noticed after these workshops that children were more engaged in literacy, developed key reading skills, and became strategic and thoughtful readers. Engagement followed in designing a learning environment where pupils' interests were used in collaborative learning settings to enable interactive social meaning construction. Enthusiasm for writing was high throughout the study, illustrating the importance of the social side of learning. There were positive effects on the instructors, who reported feeling they knew more about the subject, they were doing a better job, they had developed a more profound interest in teaching literacy, and they felt valued for their knowledge and experience.

An important feature of Kennedy's (2010) work is the idea of sustaining change through the development of a learning community. School change depends on building a community of practice to share expertise. In Irish schools, as in universities across the world, it is a challenge to find the time to collaborate and plan collectively and to reflect on the work done. However, this is essential to sustain change and to empower the instructors. Instructors need to feel trusted to share their work. Two important aspects of the professional learning community that Kennedy (2010) emphasizes are capacity building and having a research stance. Leadership in learning communities must share power, authority, and decision making with participants. The instructors found professional readings and video demonstrations of others working to be very helpful. So what was needed to facilitate these changes? In this case it was sustained professional development over a two-year period.

System-Wide Change and Professional Development

Chua (2009) gives a detailed account of ways instructors are supported in their learning communities in Singapore. In the educational sector of both primary and secondary schooling, instructor in-service training and support are very well developed. This level of support within and across schools offers a model of excellence that tertiary-level teaching staff would do well to emulate when they accept the challenge of facilitating change in practice regarding course delivery. Chua described ways instructors could organize their human resources to create instructor networks, learning circles, learning communities, and centers of excellence to promote excellence in teaching mathematics. This organization reflects the understanding that changing the way instructors teach requires structural support at various levels within the school system. The value of providing different levels of work for this type of change needs to be recognized. Instructors need ways to think about their own work and how to change it. This work is individual. However, unless it is supported it is unlikely to flourish. When groups of instructors work together, they can support one another with ideas and emotional support. Centers of excellence are an additional level of support that universities are increasingly providing. In Irish universities, over the past generation, moves have been made to provide support for teaching and learning activities. Lesson study was shown to be an effective way of doing this within the university system (Cerbin and Kopp 2006).

In terms of strategies to help individual instructors change, action research is one way that is commonly used as a personal in-class activity. Action research typically uses journal writing as a means of thinking and reflecting about teaching so that instructors can plan, teach, observe, and make notes about what worked and what did not work so well, and then critically reflect and plan for the next activity cycle. In Singapore, instructors are encouraged to introduce action research on a voluntary basis, and external agencies provide training.

However, such activities need to be more than individual. Instructors need social networks to move from personal action research to the social level to share insights and to provide support when their efforts to change are not working. It would be possible to change one's teaching using one's own classes and one's own action research, but social support will help and the power of a social network will sustain the course of personal development. Within my own institution, moves were made to institute learning diaries for students and for staff (Dublin City University 2011). These are described in the language of action research. However, this approach is in its infancy in many tertiary-level institutions. Learning diaries remain an aspiration at an institutional level in my own institution. Such activities might flourish if there were more institutional support. For example, they might flourish if they became a significant element in the normal promotion procedures. From a systems perspective, they would be most likely to flourish if the instructors appreciated that they made a desirable difference. As Fang and colleagues (2009) mention in relation to lesson study, when instructor collaboration is not part of the institution culture, there will be difficulties in establishing it. Coercive accountability procedures are likely to have negative effects.

Ways instructors could change vary, presumably depending on their readiness to change. Yeap and Ho (2009) describe four different ways that instructors change in an informal professional development program in Singapore. Some instructors ignore the program; some imitated the practices recommended; some adopted the principles; and some instructors internalized the principles of the program into their practices. Support systems as described include many elements of the constructivist perspective. The learning centers method used in Singapore emphasizes reflection and dialogue. The aim is to help schools and higher education institutions to improve and collaborate and share insights about teaching and learning in ways that facilitate community spirit among instructors.

References

Butler, D., and H. Gash. 2003, July. "Creative Learning and Spiritual Moments." Paper presented at the 15th International Conference on Systems Research, Informatics and Cybernetics, Baden Baden, Germany.

Cerbin, W., and B. Kopp. 2006. "Lesson Study as a Model for Building Pedagogical Knowledge and Improving Teaching." *International Journal of Teaching and Learning in Higher Education* 18:250–257.

Chua, P. H. 2009. "Learning Communities: Roles of Teachers Network and Zone Activities." In *Mathematics Education: The Singapore Journey*, edited by K. Y. Wong, P. Y. Lee, B. Kuar, P. Y. Foong, and S. F. Ng, 48–84. Singapore: World Scientific.

Corcoran, D. 2008. *Developing Mathematical Knowledge for Teaching: A Three-Tiered Study of Irish Pre-Service Primary Teachers*. Unpublished doctoral dissertation, University of Cambridge, United Kingdom.

Dooley, T. 2010. *The Construction of Mathematical Insight by Pupils in Whole-Class Conversation*. Unpublished doctoral dissertation, University of Cambridge, United Kingdom.

Dossey, J. A., C. O'Sullivan, and P. Gonzales. 2006. *Problem Solving in the PISA and TIMSS 2003 Assessments: Technical Report*. US Department of Education. http://nces.ed.gov/pubs2007/2007049.pdf.

Dublin City University. 2011. *Learning Innovation Unit*. www.dcu.ie/ovpli/teu/learn-tech/index.shtml.

Dwyer, B. 2010. *Scaffolding Internet Reading: A Study of a Disadvantaged School Community in Ireland*. Unpublished doctoral dissertation, University of Nottingham, United Kingdom.

Fang, Y., C. K. Lee, and B. S. Sharifah-Thalha. 2009. "Lesson Study in Mathematics: Three Cases from Singapore." In *Mathematics Education: The Singapore Journey*, edited by K. Y. Wong, P. Y. Lee, B. Kuar, P. Y. Foong, and S. F. Ng, 104–129. Singapore: World Scientific.

Gash, H. 2009. "What You Always Wanted to Know about Constructivist Education: Review of 'Constructivist Instruction: Success or Failure?' edited by Sigmund Tobias and Thomas M. Duffy." *Constructivist Foundations* 5:64–65.

Good, T., C. Mulryan, and M. McCaslin. 1992. "Grouping for Instruction in Mathematics: A Call for Programmatic Research on Small-Group Processes." In *Handbook of*

Research on Mathematics Teaching and Learning, edited by D. Grouws, 165–196. New York: Macmillan.

Gresalfi, M. S., and F. Lester. 2009. "What's Worth Knowing in Mathematics?" In *Constructivist Instruction: Success or Failure?*, edited by S. Tobias and T. M. Duffy, 264–290. New York: Routledge.

Hershkowitz, R., B. Schwartz, and T. Dreyfus. 2001. "Abstraction in Context: Epistemic Actions." *Journal for Research in Mathematics Education* 32:195–222.

Ireland. 1971. *Primary School Curriculum: Teacher's Handbooks*. 2 vols. Dublin: Stationery Office. www.ncca.ie/uploadedfiles/Curriculum/Intro_Eng.pdf.

Ireland. 1999. *Primary School Curriculum*. Dublin: Stationery Office. www.ncca.ie/uploadedfiles/Curriculum/Intro_Eng.pdf.

Kaur, B., Y. B. Har, and M. Kapur. 2009. *Mathematical Problem Solving Yearbook 2009*. Singapore: Association of Mathematics Educators.

Kelly, A. E. 2008. "Reflections on the National Mathematics Advisory Panel Final Report." *Educational Researcher* 37:561–564.

Kennedy, E. 2010. "Improving Literacy Achievement in a High-Poverty School: Empowering Classroom Teachers through Professional Development." *Reading Research Quarterly* 45:384–387.

Kreis, S. 2009. *Lectures on Twentieth Century Europe*. www.historyguide.org/europe/lecture15.html.

Larochelle, M., and J. Désautels. 2011. "The Science Wars Go Local: The Reception of Radical Constructivism in Quebec." *Constructivist Foundations* 6:250–255.

Lyons, M., K. Lynch, S. Close, E. Sheerin, and P. Boland. 2003. *The Teaching and Learning of Mathematics in Social Context*. Dublin: Institute of Public Administration.

Mason, J. 2008. "Making Use of Children's Powers to Produce Algebraic Thinking." In *Algebra in the Early Grades*, edited by J. J. Kaput, D. W. Carraher, and M. L. Blanton, 57–94. Mahwah, NJ: Lawrence Erlbaum Associates.

OECD. 2011. "Building a High-Quality Teaching Profession: Lessons from around the World." www2.ed.gov/about/inits/ed/internationaled/background.pdf.

Piaget, J. 1970. "Piaget's Theory." In *Carmichael's Handbook of Child Development*, edited by P. H. Mussen, 703–732. New York: John Wiley & Sons.

Piaget, J. 1973. *To Understand Is to Invent*. New York: Viking Press.

Plowden Report. 1967. *Children and Their Primary Schools*. London: Her Majesty's Stationery Office.

Rowland, T. 1992. "Pointing with Pronouns." *For the Learning of Mathematics* 12:44–48.

Rowland, T. 1995. "Hedges in Mathematics Talk: Linguistic Pointers to Uncertainty." *Educational Studies in Mathematics* 29:327–353.

Rowland, T., P. Huckstep, and A. Thwaites. 2005. "Elementary Teachers' Mathematics Subject Knowledge: The Knowledge Quartet and the Case of Naomi." *Journal of Mathematics Teacher Education* 8:255–281.

TIMSS. 1995. *Third International Maths and Science Study*. www.iea.nl/timss1995.html.

TIMSS. 2007. *Trends in International Mathematics and Science Study: TIMSS 2007 Results*. nces.ed.gov/timss/results07.asp.

Tobias, S., and T. Duffy. 2009. *Constructivist Instruction: Success or Failure?* New York: Routledge.

von Foerster, H. 2003. *Understanding Understanding*. New York: Springer.

von Glasersfeld, E. 1987. *The Construction of Knowledge*. Seaside, CA: Intersystems.

Wang, J., and E. Lin. 2005. "Comparative Studies on U.S. and Chinese Mathematics Learning and the Implications for Standards-Based Mathematics Teaching Reform." *Educational Researcher* 34:3–13.

Wong, K. Y., P. Y. Lee, B. Kuar, P. Y. Foong, and S. F. Ng, eds. 2009. *Mathematics Education: The Singapore Journey*. Singapore: World Scientific.

Yeap, B. H., and S. Y. Ho. 2009. "Teacher Change in an Informal Professional Development Programme: The 4-I Model." In *Mathematics Education: The Singapore Journey*, edited by K. Y. Wong, P. Y. Lee, B. Kuar, P. Y. Foong, and S. F. Ng, 48–84. Singapore: World Scientific.

HUGH GASH is professor emeritus in educational psychology at St. Patrick's College, Dublin City University, Ireland.

2

This chapter explores the ways in which a relational understanding of the educational process might inform and transform university teaching.

Relational Intelligence and Collaborative Learning

Sheila McNamee, Murilo Moscheta

Education, within a postmodern perspective, is a revolutionary act. It is not the mere reproduction of established ideas or the inculcation of social norms. It is, rather, a generative process in which knowledge is constructed, not only learned or achieved. It is a creative engagement in social transformation, not only understanding the world in which we live. Postmodern education attempts to create practices whereby people become authors of their stories, develop reciprocal relations with others, and act in transformative ways (Freire 1970). And, in a world of social and cultural differences, this approach to education must also be an act of resistance.

Therefore, learning is something teachers create with their students—a process by which both students and teachers are transformed. In a world that is dominated by traditional, modernist pedagogies, speaking about a teacher's and a student's transformation may sound radical and problematic. Teachers are often viewed as the experts and the only "transformation" is seen as teaching "improvement" through experience. Similarly, students are viewed as "those in need of learning" and their transformation is seen as achievement of knowledge and competencies. Students' transformation is traditionally evaluated with the production of disembodied markings on computer-generated examinations where they demonstrate their ability (mostly) to memorize decontextualized information. Such a view of education is based on traditional assumptions of objective knowledge, information transmission, and educators' professional expertise.

But in a world of increasing access and never-ending information offerings, technology has far more power in proliferating ideas than any teacher could ever have. Thus, educators must be challenged to go beyond the simple delivery of information and knowledge and embrace what technology is still very limited in proposing. Educators are called to take their place as relational architects.

NEW DIRECTIONS FOR TEACHING AND LEARNING, no. 143, Fall 2015 © 2015 Wiley Periodicals, Inc.
Published online in Wiley Online Library (wileyonlinelibrary.com) • DOI: 10.1002/tl.20134

In this chapter, we explore the ways a relational understanding of the educational process might inform and transform university teaching. We offer a brief review of contemporary education to create the context of our discussion. Then, using the concepts of dialogue and "communities of intelligibility," we present a way of understanding the educational process as a transformative one. Finally, we discuss the resources for action that these concepts might inspire as they are put into action in creating more collaborative educational contexts. We assume that a truly transformative educational process takes place when educators are relationally engaged with their students. Additionally, we assume that to be relationally engaged demands a reflective exploration of one's own values and taken-for-granted ideas about education, learning, and knowledge generation.

Education as a Process of Social Construction

What we take as transformative education is informed by social constructionism (Gergen 2009a, 2009b; McNamee and Gergen 1999) where learning is described as a relational achievement. Social constructionism is premised on the following (Gergen 2009a):

> The way in which we understand the world is not required by "what there is." (5)
>
> The ways in which we describe and explain the world are the outcomes of relationship. (6)
>
> Constructions gain their significance from their social utility. (9)
>
> As we describe and explain, so do we fashion our future. (11)
>
> Reflection on our taken-for-granted worlds is vital to our future well-being. (12)

As we can see, to the social constructionist, we create and maintain meaning in relation to other people. Since meaning and knowledge are by-products of relations, neither can be merely conveyed from one mind to another. The implications of this orientation for education are significant. Now, education is conceptualized as a creative process in which educators and students engage in relations that collaboratively produce meaning. This perspective is aligned with Paulo Freire's (1970) ideas and the distinction he makes between "banking" and problem-solving education, where "banking" presumes that educators/teachers "deposit" information into the minds of students (who are the depositories). Problem-solving education, on the other hand, refers to a view of where students and teachers engage in dialogue, becoming collaborators in the construction of knowledge. Freire (1970, 67) says further that "no one teaches another, nor is anyone self-taught."

One important implication of this perspective is that it requires that we replace our emphasis on individuals and their internal motivations,

NEW DIRECTIONS FOR TEACHING AND LEARNING • DOI: 10.1002/tl

intentions, and perceptions with an emphasis on the coordinated activities of people engaging with one another. The process of teaching, as well as the teaching relationship, takes center stage, and attention to the content of what people do or say recedes as our major focus. Once knowledge is viewed as a collaborative construction, it is seen as a relational achievement, not a private, cognitive process. To the social constructionist, abstract information cannot be transmitted or internalized. Rather, what we take to be information (e.g., knowledge and meaning construction) is relationally accomplished as people coordinate actions to produce meaning that is deeply connected to their histories. Therefore, knowledge is not merely accumulated in the mind of an individual; it is generated in the constant embodiment of people relating with each other.

Because this educational process transcends traditional cognitive engagement of its participants, we prefer to address it as transformative. We talk about transformation in two aspects. First, there is the transformation necessary for addressing the active involvement of all participants in the production of knowledge. This is the transformation from the traditional hierarchical "banking" model to a collaborative orientation to education. Put otherwise, knowledge is the by-product of the continual coordination of meaning among educators and students. In their attempts at coordination, all are challenged to entertain different ideas, meanings, and understandings. The second form of transformation is the move toward recognition that the knowledge that emerges from coordination among educators and students creates an understanding whereby the world can be seen anew. Education is a transformative process to the extent that people are transformed as they relate (coordinate) and, at the same time, their processes of relating transform the way they understand the world. This orientation to education differs significantly from traditional orientations toward and practices within education.

Educational Traditions.   There are many illustrations of alternative forms of education. Despite this wide array of experimental programs, it seems that schools, teaching, learning, and education overall remain within the dominant individualist discourse of our culture. We need only look to the common and expected practices within education. The focus is on individual students and their individual comprehension, ability, and performance. Standardized tests help us gauge how each individual measures up compared to the majority of age or level peers. These educational traditions emerge when the unquestioned focus of learning is on self-contained individuals (Macpherson 1962; Sampson 2008). We channel our efforts, in education, to the sole learner, and we judge knowledge and ability only of singular persons. When we look into the dominant activities that constitute what we call education, we see forms of practice that are conducive to conveying knowledge, thereby providing mechanisms to support our already existing structures (specifically, our educational system and the political and economic aspects of that existing system). This tradition is predicated on the hope that education will serve as a stabilizing institution creating the sort of people who will fit into our already existing world.

What institutionalized education ignores is the constructive possibility of education. The institution of education should be recognized as transformative, as one that creates the world. We educate children so that they can learn not only how to live in the world but how to create the future. We educate adults to provide them with resources for becoming engaged citizens. Yet, when we treat teaching/learning as a domain where knowledge is delivered or dispatched to the unknowing mind, we imply that one mind has knowledge while another does not. Our argument for the relational construction of knowledge and a concomitant transformation in educational practice draws much support from Holzman's argument. Holzman (1997, 5–6) says, "a model of human understanding that is based on knowledge, that is, on knowing x about y—is education's chief structural defect. ... Might it be that the overidentification of learning and teaching with the production, dissemination, and construction of knowledge is at the root of school failure, teacher discontent, and school mismanagement?"

Holzman's argument hinges on movement away from epistemological issues (e.g., issues of what knowledge is and, relatedly, what learning and teaching are) toward embodied activities. Embodied activities refer to those visceral ways in which we move others and are moved by them in conversation. We are talking about more than verbal or nonverbal aspects of our interactions. We are talking about those bodily experiences that also shape and are shaped by our relations with others. We share Holzman's sentiments and focus our argument on how refiguring teaching, and consequently learning, as a collaborative activity might open new forms of practice. Can we invite others into generative and transformative conversations where we create what counts as knowledge together?

There are several implications for learning and teaching when we speak of knowledge as emerging within communities of people working together. There is no uniformly right way to learn or teach. There is no universal codification of knowledge. Knowledge will vary from community to community. Various pedagogical theories, for example, will generate different understandings of what counts as knowledge and, concomitantly, what counts as an adequate demonstration of learning (or teaching). These judgments, in turn, will have serious implications for professional practice, and the conversations that take place in different learning contexts will vary, thereby expanding what counts as knowledge, as effective learning, or as good teaching.

Thus, education is not defined by a specific formula. With no predetermined formula to follow, how might we proceed in the doing of education? Can we begin to consider forms of teaching as relational performances engaging both teacher and students? When we do, teaching becomes a joint activity where new resources for action emerge. How can we engage in teaching such that we approach it as a form of practice, an activity, a conversation rather than a technique for conveying knowledge?

Relational Intelligence. Informed by social constructionism (Gergen 2009a, 2009b; McNamee and Gergen 1999), we adopt a relational understanding where education is viewed as connected to the lives of educators and students, and thus is not viewed as neutral. We share our view of education with Lave and Wenger (1991) who argue that learning should not be viewed as the transmission of information but as a process of constructing knowledge (and values) in community. Values are important for us because they play a key role in the construction and regulation of knowledge. We understand that the most important aspect of learning is how it is described, narrated, and organized within interactions that are always permeated by socially and culturally constructed values. Such understanding allows us to consider knowledge from the vantage point of its cultural and mutable meanings, avoiding essentialized (and static) approaches. Knowledge is socially, historically, and contextually produced. This means that it is not a stable and universal phenomenon that is simply presented or discussed in school settings. It is also produced there, in the interactions and descriptions that permeate in the classroom relations. Thus, the very matter of education cannot be properly addressed if the presentation of what counts as knowledge neglects the elements involved in its production and regulation.

However, as we discussed earlier, traditional approaches to education seem to be organized around the idea that knowledge is stable and cumulative. Knowledge in this tradition is a product that can be distributed among a community of students, who are then expected to uniformly receive it. The relation between the individualistic values of modernism and the educational expectancy of homogeneous learning may look, at first, like a contradiction. After all, if people are seen as independent entities, why should we expect them to behave as equals in their relation to knowledge? The modernist view is that, although separate and independent individuals, each person (student) relates to a world that is represented in terms of true or false assumptions. This is based on the taken-for-granted notion that there is (or could be if only we had the "correct" tools for discovery) one single and "True" representation of reality. The method by which an educator teaches is viewed, in this approach, as a controlled way to guide students' reasoning so that they can achieve the Truth. Therefore, homogeneity of knowledge is an expectation within an epistemological tradition that takes Truth as the ultimate goal of knowledge.

Where homogeneity is a characteristic of modern education, diversity or multiplicity becomes the trademark of a relational approach. Modernist education is concerned with conveying the one and only Truth or correct knowledge. The relational approach, on the other hand, is focused on coordinating a multiplicity of locally and communally constructed truths. We believed that the possibilities of coordination are expanded when educators are aware of the social processes that generate, maintain, and transform local beliefs. We see knowledge as a set of coordinated agreements that become coherent within a specific community of intelligibility, with its unique assumptions and values. In contemporary times, a myriad of different communities coexist and generate different and often incommensurate values that, at the same time, are always intelligible within their communities of origin.

In this relational, process-oriented view of education, the job of educators is to create contexts where different intelligibilities can be coordinated. This requires a relational sensibility where all participants (students and teachers) can become genuinely curious about diverse beliefs and values, exploring the ways in which each intelligibility is coherent within its own context. In this view, the educator attempts to create a space where multiple intelligibilities can be voiced and respectfully heard. This requires relational engagement and an appreciation for the collaborative ways in which values and beliefs (meanings) are made.

The Process of Constructing Local Intelligibilities.   The creation of values and beliefs emerges, as we have said, from a process of coordination. We might think, for example, of the first encounter between a teacher and a student. As the teacher enters the classroom, both student and teacher understand that the topic of conversation is focused on the student's academic abilities—the teacher questions and the student answers. From these collaborations, patterns and rituals quickly emerge (McNamee 2007b, 2014). Some teacher–student relationships might include questions that solicit a student's input on certain topics being discussed. The seasoned student might anticipate being asked for his or her input. These rituals generate a sense of standards and expectations that we use to assess our own and others' actions. Thus, if the teacher fails to ask about the student's ideas, the student might feel slighted or disrespected. Similarly, if the student fails to answer the teacher's questions, the teacher might feel that the expectations for the situation have been violated. Once these standardizing modes are in place, we see the generation of more global values and beliefs (i.e., social realities). We are left with an unquestioned set of assumptions about, in this case, how a learning encounter should go.

Beliefs and values are, in their turn, the basis from which new coordination can emerge. In other words, the beliefs and values that emerge from processes of coordination create what we are referring to as local intelligibilities. These local intelligibilities orient us within our future interactions, a process illustrated in Figure 2.1. We use this image to think about the production and reproduction of values and beliefs (local intelligibilities) as they inform the performances of learning (what we do when we learn; what is learning) and knowledge acquisition among students.

Figure 2.1 is offered only as a resource for understanding how the apparently simple process of coordination among people can generate entire belief systems and, in turn, how those belief systems might go on to shape

Figure 2.1. The Construction of Realities

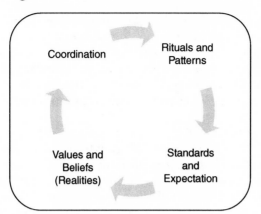

the construction of further forms of knowing (and understanding). Making sense of the contextual and relational confluence of values and beliefs present in any interaction enables educators to appreciate the multiplicity of orientations and voices present in any learning context. This also helps bring into bold relief one's own values and beliefs and to recognize them not as the Truth but as one among many possible ways of knowing the world. As in any other context, the task in education is not one of producing consensus on values and beliefs—either by persuasion, by imposition, or by discipline—but one of exploring how we might coordinate differences, thereby expanding knowledge to include alternatives to the taken-for-granted understandings of our world. Coordination, encountered within a dialogic context, creates fertile ground for growth and change. Dialogue requires relational engagement. We turn now to a discussion on dialogue.

Dialogue.   The use we make here of the word *dialogue* is a very particular one. First, we understand that dialogue is a responsive activity (Bakhtin 1982). It is focused on the process of communication, on how people are talking (and acting) in response to each other, and how their responses are mutually influential.

Second, dialogue acknowledges the different values and beliefs people bring to any conversation (Penman 2000). In this sense, dialogue is radically different from debate, where communication is aimed at persuading the other or at defending a set of beliefs. In dialogue, ideas are presented in the context of lived experiences. There is an attempt to avoid speaking from abstract positions (claiming, for example, "this is wrong" or "this is good"), and, instead, there is an effort to let the participants make sense of the different communities of intelligibility from which they originate. Instead of attacking or defending ideas, participants are curiously engaged in creating meaning. Thus, dialogue is marked by openness to diverse understandings that are the by-product of coordination among participants (note Figure 2.1).

Third, dialogue is an ongoing and unfolding process in the sense that the meaning that emerges within dialogue is constantly changing and does not have a predetermined goal. Dialogue is not focused on any particular technique or content. Finally, no meaning, no conversation is ever ultimately complete. The meaning that emerges within an interaction is always open to further supplementation and thus to the construction of new understandings.

Julia Wood, drawing on the work of Bakhtin (1982), emphasizes that responsiveness is the key feature of dialogic interaction. For her, responsiveness "arises out of and is made possible by qualities of thought and talk that allow transformation in how one understands the self, others, and the world they inhabit" (Wood 2003, xvi). If we are responsive to others—particularly to others who have views that are incommensurate to our own—then we are open to critical reflection of our own commitments and beliefs. Incommensurate worldviews at play in the educational context might best be cast as the subtle opposition between right and wrong notions of what counts as knowledge, what counts as learning, and how education should be conducted. It is particularly the case within an Asian context where different ideas or behaviors are not viewed as wrong.

Therefore, a relational, dialogic approach to education requires that we shift focus from the content of what people are doing and saying (the delivery of neutral information) to the processes in which people engage and how their actions invite each other into particular rituals and relationships (i.e., the exploration of how varying values, beliefs, and "knowledges" have emerged). This is not to say that content does not matter; of course it does—particularly in the world of education. However, the dialogic focus we are proposing here encourages a pause, if you will, in our attention to content. When we emphasize process, not content, we are attentive to the ways in which we might build conversational domains where people can talk in different ways about the same (old) issues and content.

This means that our first task is to explore ways of creating a context (physical, relational, and personal) that invites participants to talk differently about how education can proceed. We believe that a focus on communities of intelligibility and dialogue, as formulated previously, can help us develop an approach to education where values do not need to be denied or oppressed. They can be acknowledged as part of human interaction, and then, as they are dialogically articulated, the possibilities for considering more complex understandings of what counts as knowledge and how knowledge is constructed can unfold. In other words, we believe that a dialogic approach in education can generate a more respectful and appreciative context—a context that allows diverse views of learning and knowledge to commingle.

Such a view of education holds certain requirements for educators. We believe that educators are called to be present in the learning context, which means that they must position themselves as participants in communities of intelligibilities and avoid speaking from abstract, totalitarian, and unanimous positions. The central aspect of a relational approach to education is that the relation happens between people as well as between people and their environment. For people to be in relation they necessarily need to be present, not as an institutionalized voice (the voice of authority—although that voice could always be a possibility)—but as cocreators of the cultural context in which they participate.

Resources in Action: A Case Illustration

In the remainder of this chapter, we offer a very particular case to illustrate how a relational orientation to education can be useful. We have selected a particularly challenging issue because we feel that, in doing so, the value of a relational, collaborative approach to education is readily evident. Our illustration focuses on a training program designed and implemented by Murilo Moscheta and Jucely Cardoso dos Santos for sex educators. The purpose was to explore issues of sexual identity because of the largely heteronormative biases endemic within sex education (Moscheta, McNamee, and Santos 2011). However, it is important to note that our main argument in the present chapter is not limited to the content of this particular illustration. We believe that a focus on processes of relational engagement generates a more democratic educational context where diversity of perspectives itself becomes an integral part of the learning process (and, of course, of knowledge creation).

The concepts of communities of intelligibility and dialogue have informed our work with groups and teams in different contexts, for example in the context of psychotherapy (McNamee 2009, 2011), communities (McNamee 2014), health care (Moscheta, McNamee, and Santos 2010; Moscheta and Santos 2010; Wasserman and McNamee 2010), and organizations (McNamee 2005). Here, we discuss the contributions of these concepts for educators, using a specific illustration focused on promoting inclusive practices toward lesbian, gay, bisexual, and transgender (LBGT) people in the educational context. The case, as presented here, illustrates constructionist theory and how we have embraced the challenge of translating it into a practice. We hope this discussion inspires the reader to embrace this challenge as well. Table 2.1 provides a list of questions that may be useful to consider when designing relational, collaborative educational programs.

Features of the Program.   The project was initiated by an invitation from the Municipal Secretary of Education of a small town in the state of São Paulo, Brazil. The request was to design and implement a short-term

Table 2.1. Axis, Principles, and Questions to Organize the Design of Dialogic Training Programs for Sexual Educators

Axis	Principles	Questions to Be Considered
Creating the context for dialogue	Dialogue is not a debate. Stories are more relevant than opinions. Acknowledge and access participants' different communities of intelligibility.	• Do the physical and material conditions of the space allow us to have a safe, comfortable, and welcoming ambiance? • Does the invitation for dialogue generate an appreciation for what participants might contribute? • Does the opening activity invite participants to be fully engaged in the conversation? • Does the activity invite people to tell their stories rather than give their opinions? • Does the activity allow the participants to assess their different contexts and communities?
Sexuality: In search of a definition	Appreciate difference. Allow curiosity and exploration instead of definitive explanation. Search for new and unsaturated possibilities for talking.	• Does the activity allow us to talk about sexuality as social and historical construction? • Does the activity invite participants to critically consider the effects of categorization? • Does the activity stimulate participants to generate new metaphors for talking about sexuality? • Does the metaphor foster the generation of new ways of talking about sexuality? • Does the activity favor an appreciative stance toward difference? Does it avoid judgment and evaluation?
Pragmatic concerns	Information must be contextually translated. Explore possibilities rather than definition of right/wrong. Give attention to the effects and repercussions.	• Does the activity present information in a way that stimulates reflexive thinking, personal engagement, and contextual articulation? • Does the activity create relatedness between educators' stories and the presented information? • Does the activity allow thinking about responses as possibilities instead of right or wrong truths? • Does the activity invite participants to consider the implications of their responses rather than the truth they may express?

training program on sexuality for educators. The proposal defined that all educators would be invited for a 10-hour program. The program would be offered during the educators' work time, but participation would be voluntary. The expectation was that the program would cover broad issues in sexuality, with special attention to homophobia and nonnormative sexuality. The aim in designing the training program was to have educators engage in a reflexive process where they could simultaneously access, reflect, and amplify meanings they had constructed regarding sexuality.

The presumption within a dialogic orientation is that the practical resources for creating collaborative and relationally sensitive learning contexts emerge when educators engage in the exploration of their own values and move forward in the understanding of the relative nature of their construction. When educators are able to see their values as contextual constructions, they became better able to entertain values that are incommensurate within their own intelligibilities, and thus they can respond in a more flexible and sensitive way—that is, beyond the discourse of "right and wrong."

Conference.   With the assumptions in place, the program design consisted of a two-hour conference with optional participation in two four-hour workshops. Fifty educators attended the conference, which was planned to encourage their participation in the workshops. The conference, organized as an informational set of presentations, featured the variety of historical and contextual aspects that could inform one's understanding of sexuality. The conference presentations were designed to appeal to educators' memories and personal histories. At the end of the conference, participants were presented with a synthesis of the challenges educators face in dealing with sexuality in the school context and with an invitation to continue the discussion in two subsequent workshop meetings. Among the 50 educators who attended the conference, 40 (divided into two groups of 20) decided to participate in the workshops. Workshops were offered at two different times to accommodate educators with different work schedules.

Three thematic axes organized the workshop activities: (1) creating the context for dialogue, (2) sexuality: in search of a definition, and (3) pragmatic concerns (see Table 2.1).

Creating the Context for Dialogue.   The first workshop activity aimed to invite the educators into dialogue. In order to prepare them to engage in this difficult task, they were asked to write their concerns and questions about sexual education on colored paper. The colored paper was indicative of the level of difficulty they experienced talking about these concerns and questions (little difficulty/green, some difficulty/yellow, and a lot of difficulty/red). This allowed for an open discussion of the concerns and questions presented anonymously. This discussion was followed by a second activity where, in small groups, using different graphic resources, the group was asked to produce a collage that expressed their perceptions toward sexuality.

These two activities emerged from the understanding that when people gather for a dialogue, they each come from a particular position or network of relationships that contribute to their thoughts, feelings, and meanings toward the topic of concern (Chasin et al. 1996). If participants want to make sense to each other, they need to speak to those positions. The activities were planned to help gauge how to be responsive to participants' needs and create a safe context for dialogue.

Second, these two activities invited the participants to present their questions and concerns, and afterward organize them within a framework that expressed their perceptions toward sexuality. The assumption was that doing so could offer the group the possibility of accessing the communities of intelligibility from which they each come. In this way, participants become contextualized; they offer stories that render a rationale for the construction of their values. By opening the workshop in this manner, the hope was to create a context where speaking from abstract positions ("It's wrong to be homosexual!") and engaging in the debate that usually emerges from these abstractions was avoided. Positions are debatable; they easily create polarizations (right/wrong, good/bad) and foster a conversation organized to persuade or defend (McNamee 2007b; Sampson 2008; Stewart and Zediker 2002). Instead of positions, participants were invited to share their stories and were stimulated to be curious about both their own stories and the stories of others.

Thus, in both activities there was no attempt to answer participants' original questions, but to create a context for the group to explore those questions together and create connections among their experiences inside and outside the classroom. There is an important difference between opening the workshop asking for their questions and, for example, opening the workshop asking for opinions on a specific issue. Once focus is placed on the relational process, we are concerned with the different effects that our questions can produce. Specifically, asking for their questions invites participants to look for what they want to know. On the contrary, asking for their opinions invites them to look for what they already know. If questions can create space for curiosity and the creation of a collective search for meaning, opinions can easily be presented as isolated perspectives that must be scrutinized or defended.

The activities have the potential to generate a complex description of sexuality that is contextually and historically situated once it is based in personal histories. Participants can see how their stories help to create what they take as sexuality. Because the activity is in a group, they can also see the variety of understandings about the same issue. The activities can favor a greater understanding of the process by which values around sexuality are generated, and they invite participants to reflect on how their own values and sexual education have informed their performances as educators.

Sexuality: In Search of a Definition.   The second thematic axis focused on giving some information about the different components of sexuality, how sexuality is categorized in social discourse, and how these discourses operate in order to stimulate or discriminate different expressions of sexuality. The previous activities were designed to generate the context in which participants could see themselves as part of a historical and social process. This historical perspective created the conditions within which to discuss sexual identity categories as contextual. Therefore, the next activity invited participants to try to define sexuality. They were stimulated to think about its different dimensions, such as body, emotions, gender roles, desires, and sexual identity.

When the discussion about categories of sexual identity is preceded by an appreciation of how sexuality and values are historically dependent, it is easier to foster a discussion in which categories of sexual identity can be understood as artificial productions. The categories are artificial in the sense that other communities/relations will very likely create alternative ideas and values about sexuality. There is no one "True" meaning that supersedes all others. Essentialist and naturalized views on sexuality can be more easily deconstructed as the social and historical production of categories becomes evident. Usually, the following step in this deconstruction of sexual identities is the reflection about the arbitrary prioritization of one category over others and the resultant oppression and stigma. When educators become familiar with these categories as social productions, they also are able to see these categories as strategic descriptions, as Foucault (1980) would say, for social transformation.

As we have learned, the power of dialogue resides in its potential to generate new descriptions about experiences that have been repeatedly described in the same way. When those saturated descriptions change, a new venue for understanding is opened and new relations and resources can emerge (Gergen, McNamee, and Barrett 2001; McNamee 2007a; McNamee and Gergen 1999). One way of promoting such transformation is to invite people to talk about a situation that evokes less intense emotion and that is less saturated by values and judgments. That was the goal when participants were invited to engage in an activity where they had to identify a favorite season as they listened to Vivaldi's *The Four Seasons*. This activity created a context where they could talk about their preferences, how they identified them, and what they thought contributed to each preference, among other things. The group was then asked to discuss sexual identities using the ideas generated by the reflection on their preferred season. The use of a metaphor (the season in this case) helped the participants discuss sexual identities in terms of their preferences, emphasizing how those preferences were a by-product of multiple, relational contexts and how they had fluid and interdependent qualities, thereby avoiding the reproduction of a hierarchy of sexuality. The metaphor of the four seasons offered a positive model to approach difference, where preferences did not need to be evaluated (as right or wrong, normal or abnormal) but could be appreciated as a diversity that enriches our experience in the world.

Pragmatic Concerns.   From this point, the workshop moved to more pragmatic concerns, which made up the third axis of the program. In the next two activities, the legal regulations and guidelines for work with sexual diversity in school, as defined in the Parâmetros Curriculares Nacionas (PCN), were presented. Since the previous activities had focused on creating a dialogic context, it was not difficult for participants to actually relate to the information, raising dilemmas and engaging in a critical and creatively reflexive exercise. Without the dialogic context in which information can be personally and historically related, the presentation of guidelines would be unlikely to be critically received. This is the fundamental difference that defines education as a collaborative, creative, and transformative process: the creation of relatedness among one's history, the interactive moment, and any given information.

Finally, the group was divided into two subgroups and asked to role-play two different problematic situations drawn from their own experiences as educators. They were challenged to create different endings for these dilemmas. Again, the aim here was to generate a complex and multidimensional understanding of sexuality that would not allow single and standardized responses. The participants were invited to produce responses that were sensitive to the different rationales involved in the situation, and at the same time they were stimulated to think of them not as the right answer or solution, but as possible responses with particular implications.

One advantage of the relational and process-focused approach that informs this project is the possibility of the approach itself to become a resource for educators; the approach could be used to evaluate educators' responses to students, for example. The relational focus allows the educator to think about his or her responses to students no longer as limited to content (good/bad, right/wrong) and invites, instead, a consideration of the pragmatic implications of different perspectives.

New Ways Forward

In this chapter, we have attempted to articulate a conceptual orientation (social construction and dialogic process) to education with a specific interest in exploring how we might prepare educators to work in more collaborative and participatory ways—ways that invite the co-construction of what counts as knowledge. This is what we refer to as "relational intelligence." It is very important to highlight that we are not presenting a technique. Our focus is on relational processes that encourage relational intelligence. We consider technique a predefined strategy that is applied in a context and/or situation. Once it is predefined, it cannot be responsive to the participants in the interactive moment. Furthermore, we agree with Paulo Freire's critique about the use of pedagogical techniques as a way of reducing and dehumanizing relations (Freire 1998). What we are offering here is an approach that we define as a set of "resources for action" that might be taken as an inspiration. These resources are constantly put to use in response to contextual and relational demands. This means that we are never doing exactly the same thing when we draw upon a particular resource. This difference is very important, for what we have been presenting here is, above all, an effort to articulate an educational approach that is focused on the process and not the content of education and learning. To that end, our illustration of sex education should not divert attention away from broader issues of educational practice.

We believe that education must move beyond any essentializing discourse of what counts as knowledge and the unquestioned presumption that expert knowledge is the most important. In order to make such a move, values and beliefs that serve as the impetus for action in the world must be explored. One way to explore the construction of values and beliefs is to create contexts where communities of intelligibility can be explored dialogically. We hope that the ideas we offer here can inspire the design of new learning environments where collaboration and a diversity of views and levels of expertise can be coordinated in attempts to make better social worlds.

References

Bakhtin, M. 1982. *The Dialogic Imagination: Four Essays*. Austin: University of Texas Press.

Chasin, R., M. Herzig, S. Roth, L. Chasin, C. Becker, and R. Stains. 1996. "From Diatribe to Dialogue on Divisive Public Issues: Approaches Drawn from Family Therapy." *Mediation Quarterly* 13:323–344.

Foucault, M. 1980. *Power/Knowledge: Selected Interviews and Other Writings 1972–1977*. Translated by Colin Gordon et al. New York: Pantheon.

Freire, P. 1970. *Pedagogy of the Oppressed*. New York: Continuum Books.

Freire, P. 1998. *Pedagogy of Freedom: Ethics, Democracy, and Civil Courage*. Translated by Patrick Clarke. New York: Rowman & Littlefield.

Gergen, K. J. 2009a. *An Invitation to Social Construction*, 2nd ed. Los Angeles: Sage Publications.

Gergen, K. J. 2009b. *Relational Being: Beyond Self and Community*. Oxford: Oxford University Press.

Gergen, K. J., S. McNamee, and F. J. Barrett. 2001. "Toward Transformative Dialogue." *International Journal of Public Administration* 24:679–707.

Holzman, L. 1997. *Schools for Growth: Radical Alternatives to Current Educational Models*. Mahwah, NJ: Lawrence Erlbaum Associates.

Lave, J., and E. Wenger. 1991. *Situated Learning: Legitimate Peripheral Participation*. Cambridge: Cambridge University Press.

Macpherson, C. B. 1962. *The Political Theory of Possessive Individualism*. London: Oxford University Press.

McNamee, S. 2005. "Creating New Organizational Realities Together—Theory Meets Practice." In *Positive Approaches to Change: Applications of Solutions Focus and Appreciative Inquiry at Work*, edited by M. McKergow and J. Clarke, 25–37. Cheltenham, UK: SolutionsBooks.

McNamee, S. 2007a. "Relational Practices in Education: Teaching as Conversation." In *Collaborative Therapy: Relationships and Conversations That Make a Difference*, edited by H. Anderson and D. Gehart, 313–335. London: Brunner-Routledge.

McNamee, S. 2007b. "Transformative Dialogue: Coordinating Conflicting Moralities." http://pubpages.unh.edu/~smcnamee/dialogue_and_transformation/LindbergPub20 08.pdf.

McNamee, S. 2009. "Postmodern Psychotherapeutic Ethics: Relational Responsibility in Practice." *Human Systems* 20:55–69.

McNamee, S. 2011. "Relational Responsibility and Clinical Ethics." In *Psicoterapia come etica: Conditizione postmoderna e responsabilita clinica* [Psychotherapy as ethics: The postmodern condition and clinical responsibility], edited by M. Bianciardi and F. Galvez Sanchez. Torino, Italy: Antigone di Torino.

McNamee, S. 2014. "Constructing Values and Beliefs: A Relational Approach to Sustainable Development." In *Including Attitudes and Values in Sustainability Development Research*, edited by J. Appleton, 27–36. Cheltenham, England: Edward Elgar Publishing.

McNamee, S., and K. J. Gergen. 1999. *Relational Responsibility: Resources for Sustainable Dialogue*. Thousand Oaks, CA: Sage Publications.

Moscheta, M., S. McNamee, and M. A. Santos. 2010, May. *Responsivity in Qualitative Health Research: Resources for Inquiry and the Development of Non-Discriminatory Health Care Assistance*. Sixth International Congress of Qualitative Research, Champaign-Urbana, IL.

Moscheta, M. S., S. McNamee, and J. C. Santos. 2011. "Dialogue and Transformation."*Educar em Revista* 39:103–122.

Moscheta, M. S., and M. A. Santos. 2010. "Inclusão e o desafio de criar formas de investigação colaborativas—um relato de experiência" [Inclusion and the challenge to create collaborative forms of investigation—An experience report]. *Saúde e Transformação Social [Health & Social Change]* 1:154–159.

Penman, R. 2000. *Reconstructing Communication: Looking to a Future*. Mahwah, NJ: Lawrence Erlbaum Associates.

Sampson, E. E. 2008. *Celebrating the Other: A Dialogic Account of Human Nature*. Chagrin Falls, OH: Taos Institute Publications.

Stewart, J., and K. Zediker. 2002. "Dialogue as Tensional, Ethical Practice." *Southern Communication Journal* 65:224–242.

Wasserman, I., and S. McNamee. 2010. "Promoting Compassionate Care with the Older People: A Relational Imperative." *International Journal of Older People Nursing* 5: 309–316.

Wood, J. 2003. "Foreword: Entering into Dialogue." In *Dialogue: Theorizing Difference in Communication Studies*, edited by P. R. Anderson, L. A. Baxter, and K. N. Cissna, xv–xxiii. Thousand Oaks, CA: Sage Publications.

SHEILA MCNAMEE *is a professor of communication at the University of New Hampshire and cofounder of the Taos Institute.*

MURILO MOSCHETA *is a clinical psychology researcher and professor at the Universidade Estadual de Maringá in São Paulo, Brazil.*

3

This chapter advocates for a more contemporary ecological neuropsychology approach, where brain-learner-environmental interactions are the focus of study, assessment, and evidence-based intervention.

Using a Brain-Based Approach to Collaborative Teaching and Learning with Asians

Rik Carl D'Amato, Yuan Yuan Wang

Clinical neuropsychology was originally developed in an effort to identify brain impairment and assist in differentiating organic (or neurological) causes of behavior from functional (or environmental) causes of behavior (Boake 2003; Hartlage and D'Amato 2008). We advocate not for the older medical model of clinical neuropsychology where problems were seen as related to the learner in isolation, but for a more contemporary ecological neuropsychology, where learner-environment-faculty member interactions are the focus of study, assessment, consultation, and intervention (D'Amato, Crepeau-Hobson, et al. 2005). In a broad sense, ecological neuropsychology can be seen as a bridge that connects the psychology of learning to the biology of the human body or, in simpler terms, linking the brain directly to demonstrated behavior (Sousa 2006). It attempts to focus both inward (on the brain) and outward (on behavior). Both of these perspectives are important when considering how and if one is able to learn (D'Amato, Chittooran, and Whitten 1992; Davis, Johnson, and D'Amato 2005). Many scholars have argued that ecological neuropsychology bridges the basic nature-nurture abyss and can address the process of teaching *and* learning (Gaddes and Edgell 1994).

With the application of clinical neuropsychology, various brain scans are widely used in medical settings to discover problems within the brain as well as how the brain functions (Witsken, D'Amato, and Hartlage 2008). For instance, brain scanning is precise and can document a change in the brain, for example when an individual has learned to read. An ecological neuropsychological approach provides a comprehensive picture of neurodevelopment, and styles of hemispheric processing or cerebral specialization tell us how an individual best learns (Witsken, Stoeckel, and

D'Amato 2008). While we typically think of considering styles of learning with only children and adolescents, these styles continue throughout adulthood. Often they just do not reveal themselves because adult learners have found ways of compensating. This chapter focuses on developing brain-based teaching that can link to styles of student learning.

Teaching and learning represent a two-way process that must involve both the teacher and the learner together. This is especially important when dealing with an Asian population, because individuals often conform to the memorize-and-test regimen, which does not allow them to collaborate with others (Davis and D'Amato 2014). In fact, many Eastern approaches to teaching usually follow what has been called the *banking model* of instruction where information is *deposited* into the learner (Barkley, Cross, and Major 2005). Consequently, if you have not memorized the answer, you cannot solve the problem. Learners may grow up following this competitive paradigm that does not allow collaboration or co-construction of knowledge.

Whatever the case, it is clear that ecological neuropsychology offers a foundation to study collaborative teaching and learning since both of these activities are intimately related to brain functioning. We know that new learning causes neural activity and increases brain connections. As displayed in Figure 3.1, the ability to learn is determined by a learner's brain (often called biogenetic factors) as well as a person's interacting within his

Figure 3.1. Factors to Be Assessed When Working from a Neuropsychological Perspective

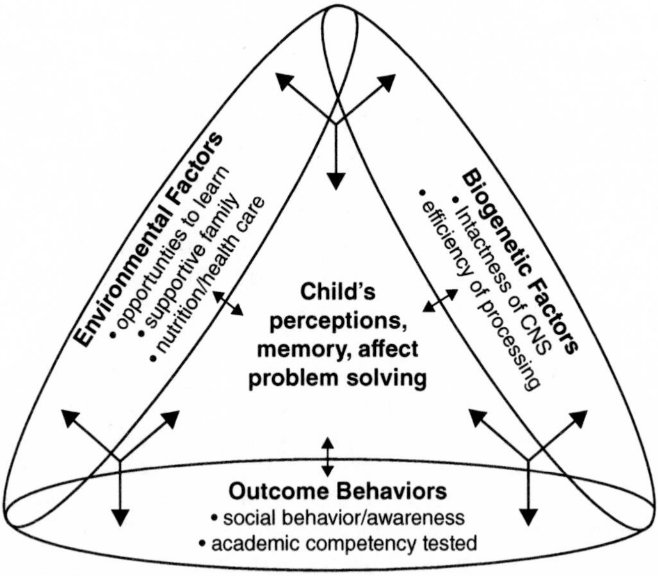

Source: Reprinted with permission from D'Amato, Rothlisberg, and Work (1999).

or her world (environmental factors). In general, 40 percent to 60 percent of learning is related to the brain and genetics, and 40 percent to 60 percent is related to environmental factors such as attending school and being tutored (D'Amato, Fletcher-Janzen, and Reynolds 2005). The neuropsychological approach to collaborative teaching allows educators to apply neuropsychological procedures in order to facilitate learning in schools and universities. This chapter also explores the advantages of why an ecological neuropsychological approach may be required if learners (as well as teachers) are to develop to their fullest potential.

Neuropsychology in an Asian Context

The question becomes whether the learner has the ability to complete the task. Understanding neuropsychology in an Asian context is critical because instructors will interact with some individual learners who, although provided with adequate to exceptional instruction, will not be able to produce sufficient educational products (i.e., behavioral outcomes). In short, they will not be able to learn collaboratively. Thus, the first job of the instructor is to determine if the student has the ability to learn in a collaborative environment. Over the years, this nature-nurture distinction has been called a variety of terms, including mind and body, mental and physical, environmental and biochemical, functional and organic, as well as neuropsychiatric and neurogenetic (Witsken, D'Amato, and Hartlage 2008). It is important to note that the instructor is *not* able to control all the variables that are related to the learner and his or her life. Figure 3.2 indicates the primary variables that could be considered when understanding a learner:

- **Content** refers to the subject area to be covered (e.g., math calculation).
- **Task** refers to the knowledge base needed to begin learning the content area.
- **Method** considers the instructional approach needed for the learner to be successful.
- **Context—Individual** refers to the unique characteristics of the learner (e.g., motivation, interests, family relationships, and peer relationships).
- **Context—Instructional** refers to the classroom-learning environment.

Some learners may have phenomenal intellectual abilities and some do not; some may be extremely verbal and pictorial while others may be quiet but analytical and mathematical. Thus, instructors must begin by understanding the cognitive or intellectual abilities of their learners. As is the case with Asian learners, as well as those from other cultures, if collaborative teaching is offered in their nonnative language (e.g., English), learners may need additional time to process the activities, and may not appear as involved in the teaching and learning process as they could be (D'Amato, Wang, and Davis 2014). It is important to separate English language usage

Figure 3.2. Instructional Areas to Be Considered When Conducting a Formal or Informal Evaluation

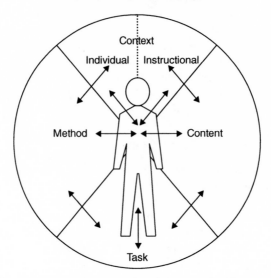

Source: Adapted from D'Amato, Rothlisberg, and Work (1999, 456) with permission.

from ability to process information, which may relate to cognitive difficulties. For instance, one group of learners may not speak in class because they see their questions as derogatory for the professor (Davis and D'Amato 2014); professors should know all, and asking questions makes them lose face. This begins to show the comprehensive nature of understanding learners and teaching in a way that they can understand. As a result, the brain could be our guide in helping understand how a student learns (Sousa 2006). As stated throughout this volume and its companion volume, the instructor must become a choreographer of learning. And this is a demanding task.

It is important in all cases to consider each of these significant learner-related areas. As a consequence, the application of *clinical neuropsychology* can be seen as a necessary way for the further study of how an individual can learn collaboratively (D'Amato and Dean 1988; Lezak et al. 2012). The neuropsychological approach is widely used for different clients and in a variety of settings, such as the assessment of learners in schools and in higher education institutions (to understand normal individuals for the discovery of strengths and weaknesses for instruction), and in medical settings (to diagnose serious neuropsychological problems) (Dean and Gray 1990; Lezak et al. 2012). According to Kosslyn and Intriligator (1992), neuropsychology provides a source of information about normal thinking and information processing. For example, as mentioned by many authors, *school neuropsychology* to some extent can be considered a specialty for the application of neuropsychology to teaching and learning in public schools, which could include a university setting (D'Amato 1990; D'Amato, Fletcher-Janzen, and Reynolds 2005; D'Amato, Hammons, et al. 1992). The clinical or school neuropsychologist can develop profiles of students that indicate how they may effectively learn. Such an approach can offer much for any university setting interested in collaborative teaching and learning and in knowledge co-construction with various populations (Barkley, Cross, and Major 2005). However, these approaches require significant advanced training in the areas of school psychology, as well as usually a two-year post-doctoral fellowship in clinical neuropsychology. Such specialists must have training in both disciplines (Witsken, D'Amato, and Hartlage 2008).

Remediation versus Compensation. There are two main ways to assist learners instructionally in any educational enterprise. The first is to determine if remedial education or compensatory education is needed (D'Amato, Crepeau-Hobson, et al. 2005). Thus, it becomes necessary to understand the definition of remediation and compensation before serving a learner. Remediation refers to the direct teaching of a particular concept to a student who may have missed learning the skill but has the ability to learn the skill. Compensation is the method applied when the individual either has lost or lacks the ability to acquire a concept or skill. In this case more teaching or practice will just frustrate learners because they do not have the ability to learn the skill (D'Amato, Crepeau-Hobson, et al. 2005; D'Amato, Fletcher-Janzen, and Reynolds 2005; D'Amato, Rothlisberg, and Work 1999). Specifically, when the required skills are age appropriate and the learner has not been taught the specific skill, remedial approaches are the most suitable and useful techniques. They may be needed when a student misses a class and does not learn a vital concept. In contrast, a learner who has been permanently impaired or lacks the ability to gain the specific skill or concept may benefit from a compensatory approach. An example of this would be teaching an Asian learner how to use a calculator if she or he could not learn math. A remedial approach is more effective when the learner is making documented progress, while compensatory approaches seek alternative ways to assist with a permanent loss or disability (D'Amato, Rothlisberg, and Work 1999).

Collaborative Teaching and Learning and Clinical Neuropsychology. We have recently seen a revolution in higher education teaching, and faculty are now called upon to help develop in their charges a number of skills that were previously not part of the educational experience. Most schools in the United States as well as in Europe have already switched from a Confucian or Socratic model of education to a more collaborative teaching and learning approach (Davis and D'Amato, 2014; Larson 2010; Witsken, D'Amato, and Hartlage 2008). But this switch is just beginning to develop in Asia. Technology is also rampant in the contemporary learning environment, and recent statistics have indicated that more individuals now use cellular telephones than have traditional toilets. This has created a learner–faculty member gap regarding the use of technology as part of daily living. Some instructors, who mostly lecture, as well as learners, who normally take multiple-choice tests, are resistant to the idea of a change in teaching and learning (Davis and D'Amato 2014). Classrooms that once were quite teacher-centered, with compliant and passive students, now have become instructional communities in which learners are actively engaged in instruction using computers, completing projects, and working in groups to solve problems (Barkley, Cross, and Major 2005; Sousa 2006).

In this changing context in higher education in Asia, the application of a neuropsychological approach is quite important; it provides data-based direction for the education of learners who could be children, young adults, or adults (D'Amato, Rothlisberg, and Work 1999). Applying neuropsychological knowledge from the laboratory to instruction can be quite meaningful. Shaywitz (as cited in D'Amato, Fletcher-Janzen, and Reynolds 2005, vii) has argued convincingly about this point: "My dream has been to see this powerful and relevant knowledge from the laboratory integrated into educational practices in classrooms and universities across the United States. We must make education a priority and implement the kinds of evidence-based treatments that are advocated in this volume." That is, to achieve significant teaching and learning, it is necessary to guide educators and psychologists to use effective evidence-based practices in the educational settings. As a result, future studies should focus on how we can apply this knowledge to Asian teaching and learning (Davis and D'Amato 2014). In addition, the application of a neuropsychological approach provides a link between assessment and intervention, in terms of matching remedial or compensatory activities to how the brain processes information (D'Amato, Rothlisberg, and Work 1999; Reynolds and French 2005). Furthermore, from this perspective, clinical neuropsychology can be considered as the foundation of psychological teaching and learning in search of the connection between assessment-diagnosis and (re)habilitaion.

In order to evoke the further development of teaching and learning in Asia, it is crucial to require cooperation and coordination among different experts in related fields and disciplines, such as professional medical organizations, university educators, rehabilitation specialists, and teachers (D'Amato, Fletcher-Janzen, and Reynolds 2005). Many previous studies have emphasized the requirement for an educational practitioner familiar with both educational systems and learning, as well as brain–behavior relationships (D'Amato, Crepeau-Hobson, et al. 2005; D'Amato, Fletcher-Janzen, and Reynolds 2005; Sousa 2006). To this end, Root, D'Amato, and Reynolds (2005) stressed that psychologists trained in school neuropsychology may be the most suitable professionals who can link medical issues with learning, since they are able to address instructors' concerns, as well as have sufficient knowledge about the learner's brain-related medical needs and expected behavioral outcomes. Sousa (2006) has advocated for a focus on the curriculum using data to adapt (and monitor) instruction to improve learner performance.

When seeking to understand a learner who has displayed difficulties in the classroom, it is necessary to collect information from a variety of avenues. Table 3.1 displays the different types of information that should be assembled when dealing with a learner who may have difficulties (D'Amato, Fletcher-Janzen, and Reynolds 2005; D'Amato, Rothlisberg, and Work 1999). Laws do require that most US universities deal appropriately with learners with special needs; they cannot be excluded.

The neuropsychological perspective provides information that can facilitate a better understanding of client etiology, and as a result, it increases the possibility of determining and dealing with learning problems, as well as preventing future academic and emotional difficulties (D'Amato, Rothlisberg, and Work 1999). As emphasized by D'Amato, Fletcher-Janzen, and Reynolds (2005), university instructors should also be able to interpret the results of neuropsychological assessments if the reports are well written and have no neuropsychological jargon, in order to facilitate appropriate academic classroom modifications. If the report is not understandable, it probably comes from a psychological or educational practitioner whom the university should not work with or should not use again (D'Amato, Crepeau-Hobson, et al. 2005; D'Amato, Fletcher-Janzen, and Reynolds 2005). To be sure, the purpose of an assessment must be to improve the effectiveness of the appropriate institutional classroom interventions.

Sequential (Successive) and Simultaneous Processing. Luria has argued for a theory of cognitive specialization that categorizes the way learners process information via three blocks of functioning (Luria 1966, 1973). In Luria's model, Block I refers to arousal, awareness, and basic life functions, and has a human energy regulation feature for the learner. Block II relates to processing style and is the most frequently researched of all three areas—that is, the receiving, processing, storage, and coding of information (Reynolds and French 2005). Both sequential/successive processing and simultaneous processing fall within this block (Das, Kirby, and Jarman 1979). Block III relates to planning, executive functions, and organization—all the higher-order human functioning (Reynolds and French 2005).

Many learners display a preference for either sequential/successive or simultaneous styles of teaching (Luria 1973). These two modes of cognitive processing are complementary rather than hierarchical. That is, they work together to create an efficient and effective manner of learning. Reynolds and French (2005) also have advocated that the examination of these two styles of processing should be a principal component of understanding how an individual best learns (D'Amato, Crepeau-Hobson, et al. 2005).

Sequential processing involves breaking the stimuli into separate parts, in order to understand what the learner is experiencing. This also involves the serial or temporal order of the stimuli. Input often is organized in a defined order (Davis 2011). The *Encyclopedia of Clinical Neuropsychology*

Table 3.1. What Areas Should Be Assessed from a Neuropsychological Perspective?

1. **Perceptual/Sensory**
   - Visual
   - Auditory
   - Tactile/kinesthetic
   - Integrated

2. **Motor Functions**
   - Strength
   - Speed
   - Coordination
   - Lateral preference

3. **Intelligence/Cognitive Abilities**
   - Verbal functions
     Language skills
     Concepts/reasoning
     Numerical abilities
     Integrative functioning
   - Nonverbal functions
     Receptive perception
     Expressive perception
     Abstract reasoning
     Spatial manipulation
     Construction
     Visual perception
     Integrative functioning

4. **Executive Functioning/ Attention**
   - Sustained attention
   - Inhibition
   - Shifting set
   - Problem solving

5. **Memory**
   - Short-term memory
   - Long-term memory
   - Working memory
   - Retrieval fluency

6. **Communication/ Language Skills**
   - Phonological processing
   - Listening comprehension
   - Expressive vocabulary
   - Speech/ articulation
   - Pragmatics

7. **Academic Achievement**
   - Preacademic skills
   - Academic skills
     Reading decoding
     Reading fluency
     Reading comprehension
     Arithmetic facts/ calculation
     Social studies
     Language arts
     Science
     Written language

8. **Personality/Behavior/ Family**
   - Adaptive behavior
     Daily living
     Development
     Play/leisure
   - Environmental/ social
     Parental/family
     School environment
     Peers
     Community
   - Student coping/ tolerance
   - Family interpersonal style

9. **Educational/ Classroom/ Environmental**
   - Learning environment fit
   - Peer reactions
   - Community reactions
   - Teacher/staff knowledge
   - Learner competencies
   - Teacher/staff reactions
   - Classroom dispositions

Source: Adapted from Witsken, Stoeckel, and D'Amato (2008) with permission.

(Kreutzer, DeLuca, and Caplan 2011, 2262) defines sequential (successive) processing as follows: "The perception of stimuli in sequence and the subsequent production of information in a specific arrangement fall under successive processing. ... Thus, information can only be comprehended in a temporal, sequential manner, with each piece being dependent on the preceding element." For example, when teaching reading, the word *cat* could be broken into three segments, with *c* listed on one card, *a* listed on the second card, and *t* listed on the final card. This style of processing is similar to what has been seen as teaching reading phonetically (D'Amato, Crepeau-Hobson, et al. 2005). Some have used the term *serial* to describe this approach, often seen as residing in the left hemisphere.

The *simultaneous processing* method, in contrast, is holistic and synchronized. Information is considered together, in its entirety, or as a whole. This approach involves spatial integration of the stimuli, organized simultaneously, and then integrated into a whole (Davis 2011). These functions are seen as residing in the right hemisphere. Kreutzer, DeLuca, and Caplan (2011, 2301) define simultaneous processing as "the process of combining discrete and unconnected stimuli into a single group or whole to assist in comprehension and interpretation. It involves the comprehension of the relationships of and between separate entities and its relation or position to the whole." An example of simultaneous processing would be teaching reading by emphasizing the shape of the word *cat*. It would be important to emphasize how the three letters are linked and shaped. Thus, people who use this processing style may be able to look at the shape of a word and tell that it is spelled incorrectly.

Besides this physiological division of the brain areas, Luria (1973) proposed the dynamic localization of the brain, which has suggested that both specific localized regions of the brain and functional systems within the brain determine the development and maturation of behavior, and operate in conjunction with each other to help individuals learn. Luria postulated three neuropsychological zones to assist in the understanding of dynamic localization. The first primary projection block is in charge of receiving and transferring sensory input to the cerebral cortex; the secondary association block is responsible for analyzing, interpreting, and storing information; and the third block is used for integrating information from a variety of sources. To a great extent, the process of teaching and learning with Asian students involves the working of all of these areas in concert with one another to produce a learning melody.

It is essential to know that simultaneous and successive processes are neither modality nor stimulus specific. That is, although certain functions are processed more efficiently through one process than the other, any type of information can be processed through simultaneous or successive means (Reynolds and French 2005). In terms of teaching and learning, it is important to find out which type of processing is most suitable to assist the Asian student to learn. Some authors have suggested that informal tests and/or observations be used to determine which type of processing is most appropriate. Sousa (2006) has provided an informal hemispheric preference measure and mentions that similar tests are available, although no psychometric data are presented to support any measure. In addition, task demand, genetic predisposition, neurocultural traditions, the individual's level of attention to the task, and the individual's preferred means of completing the task are all factors that can change based on the cognitive processing *style* an individual applies (Reynolds and French 2005).

D'Amato and Rothlisberg (1996) have advocated that all classrooms in which teaching and learning occur should be developed around what they have named an SOS approach. They believe that all instructors should consider structure, organization, and strategies (SOS) when planning and offering collaborative teaching and learning in a well-orchestrated educational setting (see more about the SOS approach later in this chapter). While they developed this model to serve children with unique needs, it is applicable to teaching and learning with Asian students at all levels. Witsken, D'Amato, and Hartlage (2008) also differentiated the quantitative approach and the qualitative approach. They stressed that the basic difference between these two approaches is how data are collected, organized, and aggregated, as well as how student performance outcomes can be used for intervention development and monitoring. It is important to be sure to focus on learners' strengths and attempt to work around learners' weaknesses.

In order to link the assessment to the intervention, it is also important to consider the specific population of university learners. For example, an Asian learner may have efficient functioning for a college-level subject but may have great difficulty with a higher-grade-level course, due to the cerebral impairment that may not be evident until greater instructional complexity is reached (D'Amato and Dean 1988). Consequently, all neuroeducational areas should regularly be evaluated if we are to determine the need for useful interventions (D'Amato, Fletcher-Janzen, and Reynolds 2005). As mentioned by Root, D'Amato, and Reynolds (2005), the influence of developing brain structures on mental development is sequential and predictable, and the nature and persistence of learning are dependent on an interaction between dysfunctional and intact neurological systems. In other words, there is a growing amount of evidence suggesting the connection between problems in learning and neuropsychological development. When discussing the application of neuropsychology to collaborative teaching and learning, there are several crucial questions that need to be taken into consideration, for example, (1) how brain functions relate to student learning and (2) how instruction can become affiliated with cerebral operations. It is more important for the neuropsychological approach to focus on the abilities of learners rather than their disabilities or, in other words, what the learner can do rather than what he or she cannot do (Reynolds 1986; Telzrow 1990).

Neuroanatomy and the Brain

In other words, how the brain works and how learning takes place are intimately related to brain anatomy, brain function, and the biological structures of the brain (D'Amato, Rothlisberg, and Work 1999). As displayed in Figure 3.3, the brain consists of four major lobes. However, it is essential for instructors to notice that the division is relatively localized. According to Beaumont (2008), although the majority of neuropsychologists hold the idea that most functions can be assigned to a specific region of the cerebral cortex, there is not precise localization to specific cells and specific functions. The degree of localization appears to vary according to the level of brain function. Furthermore, the higher the level of brain function, the more spread out the area in the brain will be. In terms of collaborative teaching and learning, it is important to know that the highest functional processes can involve the whole brain, rather than a specific area of the brain (D'Amato, Fletcher-Janzen, and Reynolds 2005). For instance, love would not be related to a single small area but would cover a large part of the brain. However, we also know that the more area of the brain we involve, the more likely learning is to take place. Thus, activities that focus on abilities in just the parietal lobe may involve less learning than a class activity that focuses on the abilities within both the temporal and the parietal lobes.

Figure 3.3 shows the cerebral cortex from a left lateral view with the four lobes and two principal fissures (Beaumont 2008). The frontal lobes

Figure 3.3. Lobes of the Brain

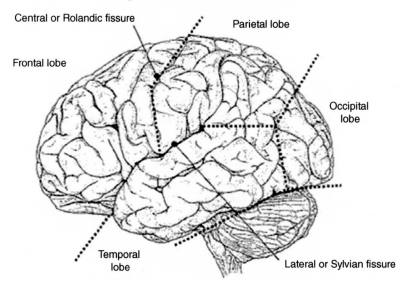

Source: Adapted from Beaumont (2008) with permission.

contain the largest portion of the brain, and are believed to include the highest mental functions, which seem to be a distinguishing factor for intelligent human behavior. The frontal lobes can be divided into the motor and premotor cortex, as well as a number of other significant areas related to language and problem solving. The temporal lobes deal with all aspects of auditory perception, with higher aspects of visual perception, and in the receptive aspect of language. In explanation, students with temporal lobe dysfunctions will have difficulties in perceiving information during the learning process. The parietal lobes process the perception of somatosensory events (relating to sensory stimuli), as well as functions with some spatial elements that combine the somatosensory information with information in other modalities. The occipital lobes form the primary and secondary cortex for vision (Beaumont 2008). Understandably, this is a critical region for success in life.

Hemispheric or Cerebral Specialization.   Various researchers have suggested that the different sides of the brain produce two independent and at times conflicting activities (see Table 3.2). However, it is crucial to note that the left hemisphere and right hemisphere actually work together in a harmonious fashion. Nonetheless, some individuals process information more efficiently when using one side of the brain. For example, when reading, one learner may be a simultaneous processor (looking at whole words), while another learner may be a sequential processor (focusing on phonetic word decoding) (D'Amato, Fletcher-Janzen, and Reynolds 2005; Witsken, Stoeckel, and D'Amato 2008). (See also the previous discussion of simultaneous and sequential processing.)

The *left hemisphere* of the cerebral cortex is specialized for language and symbolic processing, such as speech, writing, arithmetic, and reading (Davis and Dean 2005). In other words, the left hemisphere is responsible for the processes that involve symbolic communication, and it is believed to work in a more analytical, successive, linear-sequential, or step-by-step manner, rather than in a synthetic/simultaneous way (Horton and Horton 2008). The *right hemisphere* is assumed to be in charge for the perception and organization of visual-spatial stimuli, certain perceptual-motor skills, emotional functioning, spatial orientation, reproducing complex geometric and whole-part patterns, face recognition, and understanding different emotional tones and patterns of nonverbal behavior (Horton and Horton 2008). Little if any research is available contrasting Asian learner brain hemispheres with those of learners from other parts of the world (Davis and D'Amato 2014).

The Brain as a Foundation for Collaborative Teaching and Learning

The identification of a connection between the brain and learning facilitates the establishment of the foundation for neuropsychological intervention in

Table 3.2. Descriptions of the Many Words Researchers Have Used to Describe the Different Styles of Processing of the Various Hemispheres

Function	Reference
RIGHT HEMISPHERE	
Processing modes	
Simultaneous	Sperry (1974)
Holistic	Sperry (1969); Dimond and Beaumont (1974)
Visual/nonverbal	Sperry (1974); Savage and Thomas (1993)
Imagery	Seamon and Gazzaniga (1973)
Spatial reasoning	Sperry (1974); Polzner, Bellugi, and Klima (1990)
Nonverbal functions	
Depth perception	Carmon and Bechtoldt (1969)
Melodic perception	Shankweller (1966)
Tactile perception (integration)	Boll (1974b)
Haptic perception	Witelson (1974)
Nonverbal sound recognition	Milner (1962)
Motor integration	Kimura (1967)
Visual constructive performance	Parsons, Vega, and Burn (1969)
Pattern recognition	Eccles (1973)
Memory/learning	Stark (1961)
Nonverbal memory	Milner (1967)
Face recognition	Hecaen and Angelergues (1962)
LEFT HEMISPHERE	
Processing modes	
Sequential	Sperry, Gazzaniga, and Bogen (1969)
Temporal	Mills (1977); Efron (1963)
Analytic	Morgan, McDonald, and McDonald (1971); Eccles (1973)
Verbal functions	
Speech	Wada (1949); Reitan (1955); Posner, Petersen, Fox, and Raichle (1988)
General language/verbal abilities	Gazzaniga (1970); Smith (1974)
Calculation/arithmetic	Reitan (1955); Eccles (1973); Gerstmann (1957)
Abstract verbal thought	Gazzaniga and Sperry (1962)
Writing (composition)	Sperry (1974); Hecaen and Marcie (1974)
Complex motor functions	Dimond and Beaumont (1974)
Body orientation	Gerstmann (1957)
Vigilance	Dimond and Beaumont (1974)
Learning/memory	
Verbal paired associates	Dimond and Beaumont (1974)
Short-term verbal recall	Kimura (1961)
Abstract and concrete words	McFarland, McFarland, Bain, and Ashton (1978); Seamon and Gazzaniga (1973)
Verbal mediation/rehearsal	Dean (1983); Seamon and Gazzaniga (1973)
Learning complex motor functions	Dimond and Beaumont (1974)

Source: Reprinted with permission from Davis and Dean (2005, 125).
Note: References can be found in the original article; they are not reprinted here.

teaching and learning in educational settings. As D'Amato, Rothlisberg, and Work (1999) have stated, providing effective evidence-based interventions should be the cornerstone of any evaluation for a school or university setting. The following section of this chapter offers suggestions for learner interventions when teaching in higher education settings. Ornstein and Sobel (1987) claim that what a person can learn is also impacted and organized by emotions and motivation; that is, the understanding of learner motivation such as attention, relevance, satisfaction, and confidence will determine future learning (see Figure 3.4).

Using the neuropsychological approach previously discussed and the model for a learner's motivation (Figure 3.4), brain-based information can serve as our foundation for quality teaching and learning. Evidence has shown that environmental factors contribute to the development of the brain due to its developmental plasticity through numerous activities such as cell death, dendritic branching, pruning, and selecting neuronal connections, just to name a few (Lezak et al. 2012; Witsken, D'Amato, and Hartlage 2008). Furthermore, to a considerable degree, the neurodevelopment of the brain is impacted by environmental and inherited factors (Beaumont 2008; Kolb and Fantie 1997). With the help of targeted neuropsychological instruction, educators are able to design programs that are based on the specific brain ability of the learner that needs to be developed. Without such

Figure 3.4. Visual Display of the Components of a Learner's Motivation

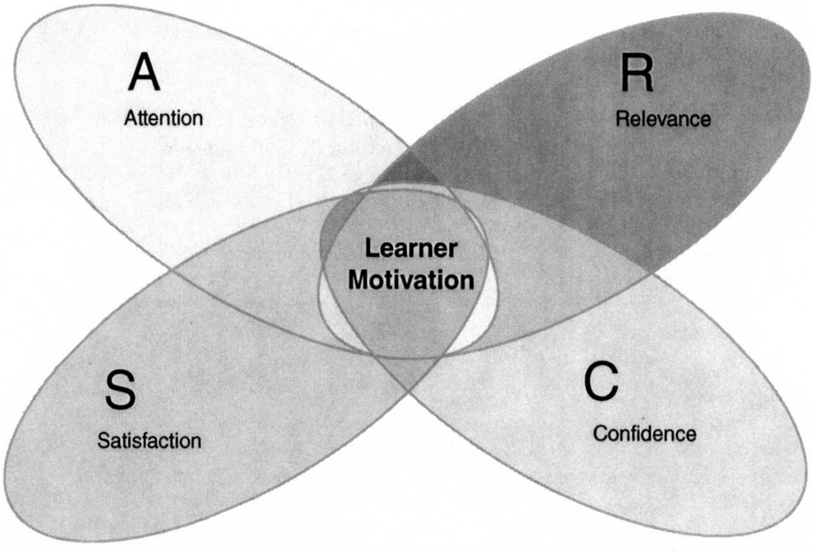

A
Attention

R
Relevance

Learner
Motivation

S
Satisfaction

C
Confidence

Source: Reprinted from the Fulton (2012) University of Macau workshop. Designed by Chris Fulton, with permission of the author.

brain-related instruction, it is difficult to identify the most appropriate and effective program for each learner. This fact also points to the importance of parental involvement during developmental years.

The neuropsychological approach is a comprehensive perspective that evaluates sensory and perceptual systems, motor functions, intellectual/ cognitive abilities, memory/learning/processing, academic achievement, communication/language skills, personality/behavior/family, and environmental fit (Beaumont 2008; D'Amato, Rothlisberg, and Work 1999). As shown in Table 3.1 and Figure 3.2, and previously discussed, *the more senses involved in instruction, the more the learner is apt to remember*. Therefore, teaching and learning are a reciprocal multisensory process, and strategies that involve more domains will allow better outcomes. This is because more areas of the brain are utilized.

All learners are different, and some have serious learning problems while others do not. Instructors must determine whether the learner has the ability to learn new skills, or will need the instructor to offer compensatory strategies due to individual difficulties (Boake 2003). Large numbers of learners drop out of university study because of undiagnosed learning problems, and a few demonstrate emotional disturbances that may contribute to significant life problems such as criminal activities or risk of suicide (D'Amato, Crepeau-Hobson, et al. 2005; D'Amato, Fletcher-Janzen, and Reynolds 2005). Many people do not realize the importance of neuropsychological factors and how these contribute to success in daily living. In terms of learning a new motor skill, the motor cortex and the cerebellum work in coordination in order to establish the pathways needed to perform the skill. Different skills develop at different ages. For instance, we expect learners to display mixed laterality until about age 9, at times using both hands for motor activities. As long as the skill can be learned, the old saying of *practice makes perfect* is true. But the skill has to be able to be learned. Nonetheless, it is critical to focus on higher-level skills as well as lower-level skills. Using rehearsal, such as simple repetition or cumulative repetition, will enhance retention (Sousa 2006). This is important for certain university classes where basic information may need to be memorized (e.g., the periodic table of elements).

It is incorrect to assume that all learners will master a year of instruction in a one-year time period. This is important for instructors to remember because a variety of students may need individualized help or choices in instruction (e.g., choosing presentations vs. papers). Ylvisaker, Szekeres, and Hartwick (1994) have suggested that since learners are progressing at their own level, it is important to arrange sequential gradation of activities according to the specific level of the individual. *Learners should not be grouped by age but should be grouped by processing or aptitude levels in most learning activities*. For example, a learner who is advanced in mathematics should be enrolled in a higher-level mathematics course.

More attention should be paid to real-world performance; that is, it is necessary to ensure that learning is shown across different environments (Boake 2003; Work and Choi 2005). Case studies, in-service trainings, presentations, and course activities should all relate to the actual tasks that learners are studying. For example, if you are instructing a class in how to teach reading, your students should receive actual practice in teaching reading (Barkley, Cross, and Major 2005). Brain studies suggest that orienting individuals to instructional environments (or educational activities) can and should help prepare them for learning (Sousa 2006). Additionally, increasing instructor and behavioral consistency is necessary in facilitating learners to strengthen their abilities and level of self-control (D'Amato and Rothlisberg 1996). Using a variety of instructional tactics, allowing modifications to learner workloads, and linking the curriculum to life skills are all very supportive activities for developing a community of learners (Barkley, Cross, and Major 2005; D'Amato and Rothlisberg 1996). Neurologically diverse learners should also have input into their learning environment, and it is critical that they learn problem-solving skills. Providing positive role models for learners, offering social skills training, and teaching a curriculum that focuses on acceptable classroom behaviors all support the process of learning, especially before beginning new course or levels of instruction.

Structure, Organization, and Strategies (SOS)

The SOS approach is described in more detail next.

Provide Structure.   Depending on the setting, Asian students may be learning in a second language (e.g., English). Therefore, it is important for instructors to provide as much structure and stability as possible, in order to minimize the students' struggling with the altered learning environment as well as to maximize their tolerance for environmental change. Any learning is difficult, but second language learners have unique challenges because they must first understand the concept, and then be able to integrate it with previous knowledge that most probably is from another language. Telling the learners in advance how the classroom time will be organized is an important teaching concept. Providing such organization in advance helps the learners to understand the structure and main points of collaborative learning activities. It is easier for them to become involved in collaborative activities when they know in advance what will occur during the class.

Forge a Home–University Partnership.   It is useful to establish a degree of contact with the home environment to communicate between the parents and university because in Asian society the link to family is vital. A university contact person can communicate with parents to offer support and help them adjust expectations for the learner. Neuropsychological links will already have been established between the learner and the family and can be used to facilitate the student's learning. Collaborative learning within an Asian context should involve parents if possible because of their serious interest in the learning process.

Increase Instructor Consistency.   Change is especially difficult for Asian students. They often memorize materials easily and give it back to us on multiple-choice tests, but that is not what they need. Learners can benefit from working with instructors who use similar collaborative styles of teaching and equivalent classroom organization. Such similarities will advantageously use brain-based connections when fostering trust, teamwork, and attachment.

Augment Behavioral Consistency.   Behavioral consistency in the classroom is equally if not more important than instructor consistency. Consistency and reliability can strengthen the abilities and self-control for learners who have difficulty following directions and making use of independent time. Clear expectations are needed for Asian learners who often look for external clues that dictate how they should behave. It is essential to offer clear rules for performance, which can eliminate confusion and increase a sense of competence for Asian students.

Control Environmental Stimulation.   Some see collaborative teaching and learning as controlled classroom chaos. Whether environmental stimulation can facilitate or repress learning is dependent on the individual student. A quiet teaching environment can aid the learning of some students, while an active teaching environment is more suitable for others. Moreover, supervision or monitoring can offer optimal learning for Asian students, who may initially have difficulty tolerating an active learning environment.

Use Instructional Tactics.   It is easier for learners to detect important elements of lessons if the instructor provides a set of routine lecture notes via PowerPoint slides including key words and concepts, and clear guidelines can be helpful. In addition, instructors may find that multimodal cues can counteract some learners' attention difficulties. Instructors should integrate learning activities that utilize vision, hearing, and tactical functions, such as having learners move around the classroom. Instructors should use as many tactical senses as possible to involve all parts of the brain. Practice with and repetition of activities, as well as feedback using live performances can strengthen learners' confidence.

Provide Role Models.   Observing peers or role models is another way of promoting learning, since the learner can benefit from both educational and social behaviors, and can receive feedback from others. In Asia, learning often takes place via the observation and copying of others. This makes the educational enterprise a challenge. It is important for Asian learners to have a role model in the classroom, as indeed much of Asian-style learning activity stems from observation of other Asian learners, and in the collaborative classroom, this must be orchestrated to move from inactive learning to active learning.

NEW DIRECTIONS FOR TEACHING AND LEARNING • DOI: 10.1002/tl

The Future of Neuropsychology

From an ecological paradigm, teaching and learning should be less concerned with determining what is wrong with a learner and more concerned with promoting what is going well with a learner. That is, professionals should focus on learners' successes, rather than on their failures. The history of neuropsychology is not long, and as a young science, clinical neuropsychology is facing a number of critics who argue that it is lacking empirical validation (Traughber and D'Amato 2005). As stressed by numerous authors, a lack of validated remedial or compensatory instructional options can be seen as the greatest problem for use with learners in the enterprise of education. Moreover, even with recent neuropsychological research findings, it is difficult to transfer brain-imaging information clearly and accurately into teaching and learning techniques. Compared to the past 30 years, recent research on brain development has greatly expanded our knowledge in this area, which allows the practitioner to have a better understanding of the relationship between neurological conditions and behavior and learning (Riccio and Wolfe 2003). As previously mentioned, many researchers have argued for the importance of applying a neuropsychological approach to learning, in order to improve instructional models as well as educational outcomes. In addition to raising the effectiveness of university instruction, a neuropsychological approach to teaching and learning can also help public schooling and improve behavioral and emotional outcomes for learners of all ages.

References

Barkley, E. F., K. P. Cross, and C. H. Major. 2005. *Collaborative Learning Techniques: A Handbook for College Faculty*. Hoboken, NJ: John Wiley & Sons.

Beaumont, J. G. 2008. *Introduction to Neuropsychology*, 2nd ed. New York: Guilford.

Boake, C. 2003. "Stages in the History of Neuropsychological Rehabilitation." In *Neuropsychological Rehabilitation: Theory and Practice*, edited by B. Wilson, 11–21. Lisse, The Netherlands: Swets and Zeitlinger.

D'Amato, R. C. 1990. "A Neuropsychological Approach to School Psychology." *School Psychology Quarterly* 5:141–160.

D'Amato, R. C., M. M. Chittooran, and J. D. Whitten. 1992. "Neuropsychological Consequences of Malnutrition." In *Preventable Brain Damage: Brain Vulnerability and Brain Health*, edited by D. I. Templer, L. C. Hartlage, and W. G. Cannon, 193–213. New York: Springer.

D'Amato, R. C., F. C. Crepeau-Hobson, L. V. Huang, and M. Geil. 2005. "Ecological Neuropsychology: An Alternative to the Deficit Model for Conceptualizing and Serving Students with Learning Disabilities." *Neuropsychology Review* 15:97–103.

D'Amato, R. C., and R. S. Dean. 1988. "School Psychology Practice in a Department of Neurology." *School Psychology Review* 17:416–420.

D'Amato, R. C., E. Fletcher-Janzen, and C. R. Reynolds, eds. 2005. *Handbook of School Neuropsychology*. Hoboken, NJ: John Wiley & Sons.

D'Amato, R. C., P. A. Hammons, T. J. Terminie, and R. S. Dean. 1992. "Neuropsychological Training in American Psychological Association–Approved and Non-Approved School Psychology Programs." *Journal of School Psychology* 30:175–183.

D'Amato, R. C., and B. A. Rothlisberg. 1996. "How Education Should Respond to Students with Traumatic Brain Injury." *Journal of Learning Disabilities* 29:670–683.

D'Amato, R. C., B. A. Rothlisberg, and P. H. L. Work. 1999. "Neuropsychological Assessment for Intervention." In *The Handbook of School Psychology*, 3rd ed., edited by T. B. Gutkin and C. R. Reynolds, 452–475. New York: John Wiley & Sons.

D'Amato, R. C., Y. Y. Wang, and J. M. Davis. 2014. "What Do We Need to Know before Serving Asian and Asian American Clients?" In *Neuropsychology with Asian-Americans: Practical and Theoretical Considerations*, edited by J. M. Davis and R. C. D'Amato, 175–186. New York: Springer.

Das, J. P., J. R. Kirby, and R. F. Jarman. 1979. *Simultaneous and Successive Cognitive Processes*. New York: Academic Press.

Davis, A. S., ed. 2011. *Handbook of Pediatric Neuropsychology*. New York: Springer.

Davis, A. S., and R. S. Dean. 2005. "Lateralization of Cerebral Functions and Hemispheric Specialization: Linking Behavior, Structure, and Neuroimaging." In *Handbook of School Neuropsychology*, edited by R. C. D'Amato, E. Fletcher-Janzen, and C. R. Reynolds, 120–141. Hoboken, NJ: John Wiley & Sons.

Davis, A. S., J. A. Johnson, and R. C. D'Amato. 2005. "Evaluating and Using Long-Standing School Neuropsychological Batteries: The Halstead-Reitan and the Luria-Nebraska Neuropsychological Batteries." In *Handbook of School Neuropsychology*, edited by R. C. D'Amato, E. Fletcher-Janzen, and C. R. Reynolds, 214–236. Hoboken, NJ: John Wiley & Sons.

Davis, J. M., and R. C. D'Amato. 2014. *Neuropsychology with Asian-Americans: Practical and Theoretical Considerations*. New York: Springer.

Dean, R. S., and J. W. Gray. 1990. "Traditional Approaches to Neuropsychological Assessment." In *Handbook of Psychological and Educational Assessment of Children*, edited by C. R. Reynolds and R. W. Kamphaus, 371–388. New York: Guilford Press.

Fulton, C. 2012. *Improving Instruction Using Technology*. Workshop presented at the University of Macau to the Centre for Teaching and Learning Enhancement, University of Macau.

Gaddes, W. H., and D. Edgell. 1994. *Learning Disabilities and Brain Function: A Neuropsychological Approach*, 2nd ed. New York: Springer-Verlag.

Hartlage, L. C., and R. C. D'Amato. 2008. "Understanding the Etiology of Psychiatric and Neurologic Disorders in Neuropsychiatry." In *The Neuropsychology Handbook*, 3rd ed., edited by A. MacNeil Horton Jr. and D. Wedding, 87–108. New York: Springer.

Horton, A. M., Jr., and A. M. Horton III. 2008. "Overview of Clinical Neuropsychology." In *The Neuropsychology Handbook*, 3rd ed., edited by A. M. Horton Jr. and D. Wedding, 3–30. New York: Springer.

Kolb, B., and B. Fantie. 1997. "Development of the Child's Brain and Behavior." In *Handbook of Clinical Neuropsychology*, 2nd ed., edited by C. R. Reynolds and E. Fletcher-Janzen, 157–179. New York: Plenum.

Kosslyn, S. M., and J. R. Intriligator. 1992. "Is Cognitive Neuropsychology Plausible? The Perils of Sitting on a One-Legged Stool." *Journal of Cognitive Neuroscience*, 4, 96–106.

Kreutzer, J., J. DeLuca, and B. Caplan, eds. 2011. *Encyclopedia of Clinical Neuropsychology*. New York: Springer.

Larson, D. 2010. *Teaching Using Technology*. Paper presented at the University of Macau to the Centre for Teaching and Learning Enhancement, University of Macau.

Lezak, M. D., D. B. Howieson, E. D. Bigler, and D. Tranel. 2012. *Neuropsychological Assessment*, 5th ed. New York: Oxford University Press.

Luria, A. R. 1966. *Higher Cortical Functions in Man*. New York: Basic Books.

Luria, A. R. 1973. *The Working Brain*. Harmondsworth, England: Penguin.

Ornstein, R., and D. Sobel. 1987. *The Healing Brain*. New York: Simon & Schuster.

Reynolds, C. R. 1986. "Clinical Acumen but Psychometric Naivete in Neuropsychological Assessment of Educational Disorders." *Archives of Clinical Neuropsychology* 1:121–138.

Reynolds, C. R., and C. L. French. 2005. "The Brain as a Dynamic Organ of Information Processing and Learning." In *Handbook of School Neuropsychology*, edited by R. C. D'Amato, E. Fletcher-Janzen, and C. R. Reynolds, 86–119. Hoboken, NJ: John Wiley & Sons.

Riccio, C. A., and M. E. Wolfe. 2003. "Neuropsychological Perspectives on the Assessment of Children." In *Handbook of Psychological and Educational Assessment of Children: Intelligence, Aptitude, and Achievement*, 2nd ed., edited by C. R. Reynolds and R. W. Kamphaus, 305–324. New York: Guilford.

Root, K. A., R. C. D'Amato, and C. R. Reynolds. 2005. "Providing Neurodevelopmental, Collaborative, Consultative, and Crisis Intervention School Neuropsychology Services." In *Handbook of School Neuropsychology*, edited by R. C. D'Amato, E. Fletcher-Janzen, and C. R. Reynolds, 15–40. Hoboken, NJ: John Wiley & Sons.

Sousa, D. A. 2006. *How the Brain Learns*, 3rd ed. Thousand Oaks, CA: Sage Publications.

Telzrow, C. F. 1990. "Management of Academic and Educational Problems in Traumatic Brain Injury." In *Traumatic Brain Injury*, edited by E. D. Bigler, 251–272. Austin, TX: ProEd.

Traughber, M. C., and R. C. D'Amato. 2005. "Integrating Evidence-Based Neuropsychological Services into School Settings: Issues and Challenges for the Future." In *Handbook of School Neuropsychology*, edited by R. C. D'Amato, E. Fletcher-Janzen, and C. R. Reynolds, 827–858. Hoboken, NJ: John Wiley & Sons.

Witsken, D., R. C. D'Amato, and L. C. Hartlage. 2008. "Understanding the Past, Present, and Future of Clinical Neuropsychology." In *Essentials of Neuropsychological Assessment: Rehabilitation Planning for Intervention*, 2nd ed., edited by L. C. Hartlage and R. C. D'Amato, 1–30. New York: Springer.

Witsken, D., A. Stoeckel, and R. C. D'Amato. 2008. "Leading Educational Change Using a Neuropsychological Response-to-Intervention Approach: Linking Our Past, Present, and Future." *Psychology in the Schools* 45:781–791.

Work, P. H. L., and H. Choi. 2005. "Developing Classroom and Group Interventions Based on a Neuropsychological Paradigm." In *Handbook of School Neuropsychology*, edited by R. C. D'Amato, E. Fletcher-Janzen, and C. R. Reynolds, 664–684. Hoboken, NJ: Wiley.

Ylvisaker, M., S. F. Szekeres, and P. Hartwick. 1994. "A Framework for Cognitive Intervention." In *Educational Dimensions of Acquired Brain Injury*, edited by R. C. Savage and G. F. Wolcott, 35–67. Austin, TX: ProEd.

RIK CARL D'AMATO *is a professor of psychology on the faculty of the Chicago School for Professional Psychology, and former director of the Centre for Teaching and Learning Enhancement at the University of Macau, China.*

YUAN YUAN WANG *is a PhD graduate from the Department of Psychology at the University of Macau, Macau S.A.R., China.*

This chapter explores emotional intelligence as the glue that binds people together regardless of cultural differences.

Emotional Intelligence and Sociocognitive Skills in Collaborative Teaching and Learning

Helen Y. Sung

The pendulum is once again swinging to Asia after approximately 400 years of Western dominance in the world (Bradley 2012). Now is the time to think about the future direction of our global world as educators and professors from across the continents have an opportunity to teach young people in Asia. How can professors bring out the best in Asian students so that they will benefit from diverse perspectives? What is the common human potential that could be highlighted to enhance growth not only academically but also emotionally? The social cognitive theory explains that humans are influenced bidirectionally as social agents in the culture in which the people function (Bandura 1996; Mischel, Shoda, and Ayduk 2008). Thus, individuals and groups have the power to create their own environment and destiny.

Higher education should prepare young people for the challenges of the twenty-first century. Yet, the goal of education for most young people in Asia is to get good grades and to secure a good job (Kember, Hong, and Ho 2008). Traditionally, the educational system relied on achievement scores to measure success. Instead of perpetuating the status quo, the educational system needs to produce students who can utilize their knowledge to solve problems often global in nature and to collaborate effectively with people from across cultural boundaries for the benefit of all people. They need to be aware of their capacity to regulate emotions, think constructively, galvanize strengths in others, and communicate to improve human conditions. The challenge of twenty-first-century education in Asia is to shift the priorities and belief systems to where emotional intelligence skills are important for higher-order cognitive functioning. The concept of global citizenship may become a reality in the next generation (Banks 2008; Stewart 2007). Thus, the ability to function globally becomes a priority.

NEW DIRECTIONS FOR TEACHING AND LEARNING, no. 143, Fall 2015 © 2015 Wiley Periodicals, Inc.
Published online in Wiley Online Library (wileyonlinelibrary.com) • DOI: 10.1002/tl.20136

Emotional intelligence is the glue that binds people together. Regardless of the cultural differences, emotional aspects of the brain function in similar ways (LeDoux 1996). As individuals connect with each other at a deeper level, a sense of understanding and commonality can be found. This chapter describes the human potential to develop emotional intelligence as explained in the Eastern and Western paradigms. The common ground can be found when investigating the definition of emotional intelligence that focuses on self-development, human relationships, adaptability, problem solving, and constructive thinking (Bar-On 2001; Epstein 1998). Higher education in Asia can increase emotional intelligence in students through experiential learning, explicit modeling, direct coaching, and relationship building.

Emotional Intelligence in the Global Context

Even though socialization processes and priorities may differ among Eastern and Western cultures, the human brain operates basically the same way when processing emotional information. LeDoux (1996) stated that most information processing occurs unconsciously and automatically. The human brain consists of neural links that send information from one to another. Information spreads through the neural transmitters to elicit processing, behavior, and emotions. All normally developed human brains function in the same way, and emotions are an integral part of neurological functioning.

The amygdala is the critical center that triggers physiological changes to emotional responses. A crucial emotional circuitry runs from the amygdala to the prefrontal area of the midbrain. The neurons orchestrate communication between the prefrontal area and the limbic circuitry (Goleman, Boyatzis, and McKee 2002). When the prefrontal lobe is inadequately developed, emotional intelligence is inadequately developed. Maté (1999) explained how the quality of the relationship between parents and child impacts the development of the prefrontal area in the early years. The first definition of emotional intelligence was defined in terms of the neurological function: The brain becomes aware of the emotions, integrates them into thoughts, understands and manages the emotions, and thus requires information processing (Salovey and Mayer 1990).

Thinking and information processing are considered the cognitive functions. Constructive thinking is a way of thinking about a situation that allows the best possible outcomes. Instead of focusing on the negative, overgeneralizing, or worrying needlessly, constructive thinking focuses on the positive side of things, views difficulties as a challenge, and moves forward instead of being stuck. By changing the process of automatic thought, it brings about change in emotional responses (Epstein 1998; Vernon 1989).

People routinely use emotions to make judgments and decisions. Although facial expression conveys judgment externally to others, emotions convey internal judgments to the self. Affect provides information about the self and social awareness. Often, the interaction between the environment and the self operates unconsciously (Gohm and Clore 2002). The concept of intelligence includes perception of information and control of output. Just as cognitive intelligence depends on information perceived by auditory and visual input, emotional intelligence processes information through perception via auditory and visual senses (Barrett and Salovey 2002). Emotional responses are triggered by the tone of voice, body gestures, and facial expressions of others (Bachorowski and Owren 2002; Elfenbein, Marsh, and Ambady 2002). Before language develops, the infant distinguishes the familiar from the unfamiliar, recognizes the caregiver's voice, imitates the facial expressions, and senses the mood in the environment.

Already at an early age, the brain begins to make neurological pathways as information is perceived through the five senses and as the infant observes and starts to interact with the environment. The environmental feedback and pattern of interaction in relationships with significant caregivers and parents impact the pattern of brain function (Maté 1999). Over time, the brain has crystallized and operates the way it is wired. For this reason, it takes extra effort, time, and energy to make new neurological pathways for emotional intelligence growth in adulthood. Understanding how the brain functions can lead to actions where higher education students in Asia use learning strategies to promote growth in emotional intelligence. The educational environment is an optimal place to practice skills that would not manifest and grow otherwise.

Cross-Cultural Relevance of Emotional Intelligence

The field of psychology and the study of the emotional–environmental link have undergone many transitions since the early beginnings in the late nineteenth century. Thorndike's (1905) *law of effect* focused on the effect of behavior and not only on the behavior itself. Rogers (1961) discussed the transformational potential of an individual that is linked to the person's environment, while Kelly (1955) stated that the person's expectation and anticipation play a central role in her or his behavior within the environment. These psychologists, as well as many others, emphasized the function of cognitive processes to understand the social world (Bar-On and Parker 2002; Mayer 2001). The field of cognition and affect studied the impact of emotion on thoughts. Furthermore, research in nonverbal communication and artificial intelligence led the way to Gardner's multiple intelligence theory (Mayer 2001). Gardner (1993) described personal intelligence as consisting of both intrapersonal and interpersonal intelligence. Intrapersonal intelligence allows a person to be introspective about her or his own feelings. Interpersonal intelligence is the capacity to detect moods of people during interactions. Self-awareness and growth in both these intelligences can lead to positive influence on others.

Eastern philosophy was saturated with Confucius's teaching. Yet, some of the basic premises of human relationship appeared to be similar to intrapersonal and interpersonal intelligences. The underlying assumption of Confucianism states that "man [sic] exists in relation to others" (Bond 1987, 215). Confucius also made the distinction between vertical and horizontal dimensions of relationships. A vertical dimension is used to cultivate the self in order to be wise and virtuous and in tune with nature or the cosmos. A horizontal dimension is used to cultivate harmony and relationships with other people by becoming a worthy person and to have a positive influence on others. Cultivating oneself can occur in two ways: through education and self-reflection (Berthrong and Berthrong 2000).

Barriers to Emotional Intelligence in Asian Cultures.   The brain is like a muscle that gets stronger with exercise. The area of the brain that is not used gets pruned away, removing less efficient neural connections (Goleman 1998; Neville and Bruer 2001). The development of emotional intelligence depends on the experiences of emotional awareness, interpersonal functions, monitoring of emotions, and the use of social cognitive information to solve problems (Vernon 1989). Learning from the social environment is described in the social cognitive theories. Experiential learning within one's cultural belief system can be linked to emotional intelligence development. The hierarchical, obedience-oriented parenting and punitive way of discipline found in Asian families can stifle the growth of emotional intelligence (Sung 2010). Discipline in Asia is often punitive at home and at school. Fung and Chen (2001) found 300 events of shaming in more than 100 hours of videotaped spontaneous home interactions. While shame may be associated with weak and incompetent members of society in Western culture, Asian cultures readily accept shame and sometimes view self-blaming and self-recrimination as virtues. This is common in collectivist cultures where gaining approval of others is highly valued.

Specifically, shame is used to create awareness of good conduct and for moral socialization, and Chinese parents believe the sense of shame is necessary before the sense of right and wrong can be developed (Fung, Lieber, and Leung 2003). Lee (1999) stated that the concepts of right and wrong or good and bad are the result of socialization in the cultural context. For example, Korean children judged their abilities and traits significantly lower than European-American children, and Korean-American children expressed more sadness and anger and less happiness than European-American children did. Moreover, shaming could lead to depression, anxiety, and suicide. Historically, suicide has been encouraged in some Asian cultures (e.g., Japan) to save face or to maintain honor (Ho, Fu, and Ng 2004; Yang and Rosenblatt 2001). In their study, Lau, Jernewall, Zane, and Myers (2002) found that depression was the major predictor for suicide among older Asian adolescents. The use of shame and guilt in a collectivist society that also values authoritarian filial piety may be the ingredient for depression and poor sense of self-worth.

Not only do the beliefs and values of hierarchy and an authoritarian parenting style impact emotional intelligence development (Sung 2010), but they also influence the teaching style in the Asian education system. Leung (2001) describes the impact of cultural values and belief systems on mathematics teaching practice between East Asian and Western counterparts. Education in East Asia is content oriented and examination driven, and promotes rote learning for immediate success and higher grade achievement. The practice comes from the belief that content is fundamental. Without the content, there is nothing to process. Memorization is considered a part of learning even when the material is not totally understood. Pleasure comes after hard work when the sense of accomplishment is felt. Learning itself may not be pleasant when challenged, but the motivation to do well on the examination may be rewarded. Examinations have played a vital role in distinguishing those who are "able" from the "less able," so competition is considered to be a fair method (Leung 2001). The belief in the importance of memorization and competition may result in higher test scores, but it can be at the expense of values related to emotional intelligence development.

Furthermore, the Asian hierarchical orientation impacts relationships because people are expected to be obedient and compliant to those in power positions. Thinking, questioning, and initiating discussion are discouraged as dependency on authority for direction is reinforced. In their early years, children are expected to wait for adults to tell them what to do. Mistakes are not tolerated, and punishment may be delivered for poor performance. In such cases, self-initiation, assertiveness, independence, and sense of responsibility diminish. As young people enter higher education, they may be knowledgeable with a great amount of information through formal schooling, but the application of their knowledge such as analyzing, synthesizing, making connections, evaluating, and applying critical thinking may be limited.

Nonetheless, promoting emotional intelligence increases higher-order thinking skills and strengthens reflective thinking, problem solving, empathy, assertiveness, and the ability to communicate effectively. Educators and professors in higher education in Asia have a huge task ahead of them to shift the paradigm from a hierarchical to a collaborative learning environment. One of the natural ways to approach the change is through cooperative project-based learning. It changes the expectation of students from receiver of information to giver of information and co-constructor of knowledge. The shared participation and listening to peers remove the focus from the instructor in a hierarchical position while encouraging the development of emotional intelligence through collaborative and attuned relationships (Maté 1999; Sung 2010).

Confucian Heritage Culture and Education in Asia.   During the political chaos in the fourth century BC, there were many challenges to Confucianism, one of which was the Legalist school of thought. Legalists thought virtue was a waste of time. They argued that people responded to pain and pleasure, and the way to establish order and control is through power and authority. They maintained that the state would flourish only if there was an organized bureaucracy with political power in an autocratic system (Berthrong and Berthrong 2000). In this context, Confucius's followers proposed the principles of the hierarchical and authoritarian society. Patriarchal authoritarianism became the common social as well as family order (Song 2002). Confucian men also transferred the same authoritarian way of ruling into the education system. In some ways, Confucius was ahead of his time given the social constraints. Only the educated elite became members of the ruling class, which made self-cultivation a very slow process for the common people. Although a reciprocal relationship was the intent of Confucianism before it evolved into an authoritarian hierarchy, elites used Confucianism to establish hierarchy and a domineering society. For generations, a hierarchical and domineering system permeated the social system, including education (Bond 1987).

Bond (1987) reported that reciprocal filial piety is believed to be more beneficial, fostering more intergenerational and family cohesion compared to authoritarian filial piety, which leads to rigidity and negative personality orientation (Yeh 2003). Older adolescents with high emotional intelligence in Sung's (2010) study experienced interaction patterns with their parents that were more reciprocal than hierarchical throughout their developmental years. Transferring this finding to higher education in Asia, developing a collaborative and reciprocal relationship between the instructor and the student can be the catalyst in the emotional center of the brain for development of the student's emotional intelligence. Instructors can encourage the development of emotional intelligence through probing for problem solving through open-ended questions, making connections to real-life experiences, and analyzing data to support arguments. Building an instructor–student reciprocal relationship and expecting deeper thinking add to emotional intelligence development.

Nurturing Emotional Intelligence through Social Cognition in Asian Higher Education

The human brain is not as static as people once thought. The capacity to develop and increase emotional intelligence continues beyond primary and secondary school. Dweck (1988) pointed out that intelligence is not a static skill but always evolving in relation to social cognition, which can be used to increase social awareness and experiential learning. According to Vygotsky's social learning theory and in the collaborative teaching and learning environment, students learn to be thinkers as they reflect and talk about their thinking. The community of learners makes it possible for students to interact with one another, stay engaged in the learning process, and solve problems (Jennings and Di 1996). The learning groups are forced to use higher-order thinking as they apply, analyze, synthesize, and evaluate each other's contributions. According to Vygotsky, learning is embedded in social events and social interactions (Wang 2006), and social cognition plays an important role in the transmission of the emotional intelligence. The awareness of self and the social interaction with others impact the neuro-transmitters to operate in certain pathways that lead to learning. For example, Sung (2010) found that the interaction pattern between parent and child over time correlated with the emotional intelligence development as measured by Bar-On's Emotional Intelligence Inventory (Bar-On 2004) and student interviews. Instructors can extrapolate from the study the type of interaction patterns that promote emotional intelligence.

A comprehensive definition of emotional intelligence seems to be an eclectic integration of major branches in psychology: (1) intrapersonal emotional intelligence—self-awareness and self-actualization found in psychodynamic and humanistic psychology; (2) interpersonal emotional intelligence—social influence and interpersonal skills found in social psychology; (3) adaptability—reality testing and problem solving found in rational-emotional psychology; (4) stress management—stress tolerance and impulse control found in rational-emotive and behavioral psychology; and (5) general mood—optimism and happiness found in humanistic and positive psychology (Bar-On and Parker 2002; Forgas 2001; Mayer 2001; Salovey 2001; Salovey and Mayer 1990). The instructor's knowledge about the specific components of emotional intelligence will guide the goals of emotional intelligence coaching, mentoring, and learning (see Figure 4.1).

Intrapersonal Emotional Intelligence.   Intrapersonal emotional intelligence is one of the five aspects of emotional intelligence consisting of self-awareness, assertiveness, self-regard, self-actualization, and independence (Bar-On 2004). The awareness and the ability to view the self and

Figure 4.1. Five Areas of Bar-On's Emotional Intelligence

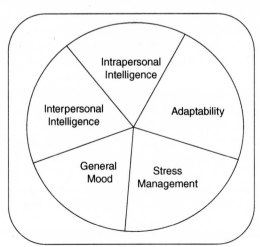

to self-reflect are skills that can be developed (Wang 2006). In order to promote emotional intelligence, time and effort should be expended to make connections between thinking, feeling, and behaving. Through reflective thinking, modeling, and discussions about their thoughts, emotions, and behaviors, students will be better able to monitor and regulate their emotions and behaviors through constructive thinking (Epstein 1998). Self-acceptance and self-esteem are based on self-reflection as well as what is reflected in the social world (Lewkowicz 1999). In a collaborative teaching and learning environment and with building true reciprocal relationships between all parties (i.e., instructor and students), assertiveness is fostered through critical thinking and engaging in discussions about different point of views.

Interpersonal Emotional Intelligence.   Interpersonal emotional intelligence is the second component of the emotional intelligence definition (Bar-On 2004). It consists of empathy, interpersonal relationships, and social responsibility. Consistent with the social cognition and social learning theory, a community of learners in a collaborative teaching and learning environment is a great way to develop empathy, as students are expected to take the perspective of others, look at the problem from different perspectives, and discuss multiple solutions instead of right or wrong answers. The culture in the classroom facilitates social cognitive learning (Kozulin 2004; Wang 2006). It also engenders a sense of belonging and a powerful motivator for higher education (Kember, Hong, and Ho 2008). Furthermore, the instructor–student relationship makes a difference between academic success and failure. Those who are actively engaged in the learning process tend to have better relationships with their instructors and buffer the negative effects of "insecure-other" attachment (O'Connor and McCartney 2007).

Sung (2010) also found that those with higher emotional intelligence had many opportunities to interact with extended families and family friends, and participated in volunteer activities. Their relationships with parents were good during all phases of life, and they felt respected because of reciprocal relationships and open communication. Similarly, Maté (1999) maintains that attuned parents are sensitive to the child's needs and promote genuine relationships, which contribute to the development of the area in the brain responsible for emotional intelligence. Relationship building not only supports the individual but also benefits people in the environment. People who are able to experience strong relationship with those in guidance roles such as parents or teachers are able to establish strong relationships with others. The instructor in higher education, particularly in Asia, needs to be mindful of building sound interpersonal relationships with the students, and this should be a top priority when developing emotional intelligence in a collaborative teaching and learning environment.

Adaptability.   The third component of emotional intelligence is adaptability, which includes problem solving and reality testing (Bar-On

2004). Ultimately, the goal of emotional intelligence is to be able to solve personal and communal problems. All people face problems, and dealing with them is an integral part of life's journey. The ability to read nonverbal cues, anticipate problems, be flexible, and make decisions enhances problem-solving skills. These skills are not taught explicitly but may be the outcome of experiential learning and high emotional intelligence.

Sung (2010) found distinct differences in attitude and perception between those with very low emotional intelligence and those with high emotional intelligence. Participants with very low emotional intelligence are greatly impacted by the opinions of others. They avoid problems by escaping and generally cannot identify any problems but will rather avoid or deny. Low emotional intelligence keeps people stuck in their problems because they may not be aware of the problems. They have poor self-images or pessimistic views of life, and do not have goals and dreams, thinking that having a goal will not matter because others will knock it down. Their black-or-white perception leads to an all-or-nothing mind-set, as they perceive things (also learning) as either all good or all bad. Once faced with failure, these individuals perceive their entire life as a failure, and being more vengeance-oriented, they want to even the score when they have been offended. Furthermore, people with low emotional intelligence are more likely to suffer from mental illness (Taylor 2001), and less likely to seek help (Ciarrochi, Deane, and Wilson 2002).

In contrast, participants with high emotional intelligence are able to identify problems (Sung 2010). They can describe the scenario of the problem and find a way to solve the problem, and are self-confident and optimistic as they take ownership of the situation, act assertively to address the problem, and believe in their own ability to solve problems. These participants are able to have a perspective and manage their emotions through self-reflection and thinking about what could be done better. They are also flexible and able to adapt to young or old, familiar or unfamiliar, and difficult or easy-going people. For these participants, positive relationships further foster adaptability in the educational environment. They are able to accept the academic responsibilities, complete projects, meet deadlines, and have organizational skills. A collaborative teaching and learning environment encourages such positive relationships and the development of assertiveness and problem-solving skills.

Stress Management.   The fourth component of emotional intelligence is stress management, consisting of stress tolerance and impulse control (Bar-On 2004). The characteristics of those with high emotional intelligence are emotional resilience, acceptance of self and others, open expression of feelings, and making decisions based on both feeling and logic to manage stress and to control impulses. Saarni (2000) discusses the consequences of emotional competence as coping, emotional management, and well-being. Students who are emotionally competent also have social support to obtain effective help with coping in stressful situations (Taylor 2001).

General Mood. The fifth area of emotional intelligence is general mood such as happiness and optimism (Bar-On 2004). When emotional intelligence increases, relationships are built, goals are set, and success is recognized, while the individual's thoughts, emotions, and behaviors reflect positive interactions and outcomes, ultimately leading to a sense of optimism and happiness. Nonetheless, emotional intelligence is not a magic formula or set of guidelines for optimal performance in the learning environment. Rather, it is the way that the brain functions when utilizing internal and external resources in a collaborative teaching and learning environment. Certain patterns of interactive behaviors trigger the brain function that connects emotional intelligence with social cognitive learning (LeDoux 1996; Matsumoto 1997; Wang 2006), and in the higher education setting in Asia, this could be transformed into optimizing learning for all involved.

The interaction patterns with the instructor and peers that provide opportunities for reflection, feedback, relationship building, and cooperative or group projects are important aspects of social cognition. In the collaborative teaching and learning environment, the dynamics of interaction need to be brought to attention purposefully. The interaction processing may not be easy at first, but in order to create a culture of social cognitive thinkers, the connections among thinking, feeling, and behaving must be made. Information sharing and respect for ideas must be bidirectional, not hierarchical. As students are given more opportunity to think critically, plan, organize, evaluate, create, make choices, and give feedback, the area of the brain that operates on emotional intelligence will continue to develop (Sung 2010). Therefore, instructors could promote emotional intelligence by focusing on social interaction patterns, modeling empathy, and being present with the students.

Coaching and Mentoring

Emotional intelligence is for every human being and not just for people who happen to have the optimal circumstances with parenting, cultural norms, expectations, and skills. Emotional intelligence can be developed as the brain continues to grow and learn (Goleman 1995). Promoting emotional intelligence in higher education in Asia is appropriate because it is a training ground for future professionals and parents as well as leaders in educational settings (Moore 2009; Vandervoort 2006).

Self-reflection refers to the ability to become aware of one's belief systems and is critical, as all behaviors begin with one's thought and values. As educators understand their own strengths and weaknesses in all five areas of emotional intelligence described earlier, progress can be made. Yet people's underlying assumptions can be the barriers to emotional intelligence development. Sung (2013) compiled a training workbook to help adults reflect on their own socialization process such as their belief systems, extended families, early experiences, and modeling. Only after self-reflection and recognizing one's own emotional intelligence level is the instructor ready to serve as coach in the higher education setting.

Lewkowicz (1999) described techniques to explicitly teach emotional intelligence. First, relate the concepts of self-awareness, emotional management, relationship building, empathy, self-skills, and self-control in an age-appropriate manner. Second, invite the participants to describe the situation they can relate to in each of the topic areas. Third, challenge assumptions by role-playing the scenarios with barriers. Fourth, change the assumptions to more constructive thinking, and role-play the function of emotional intelligence. Each of the areas could be a broken down into several lessons with discussions, reflections, and analysis. The following are the specific areas of emotional intelligence teaching:

- *Self-acceptance*—change self-defeating thoughts and enhance personal power.
- *Recognizing feelings*—be aware of defense mechanisms and own your emotions.
- *Beliefs and behaviors*—identify values and self-defeating behavior.
- *Problem solving/decision making*—use problems as opportunities and put things in perspective looking at the bigger picture.
- *Interpersonal relationships*—recognize the connection between negative feelings toward others and irrational beliefs.

Vernon (1989) uses sample scenarios to prompt discussions and activities around identified themes. At first the discussion is impersonal when talking about a sample situation with no specific names mentioned, and then students are asked to identify with the scenario in their own lives. Connections are made between a thematic topic, sample scenarios, and personal experiences related to the topic.

Teaching emotional intelligence explicitly may not be enough when it is not implemented in all areas, because people do not function in isolation. The academic culture promotes emotional intelligence when the provost, dean, and directors value social and emotional intelligence learning. Pasi (2001) stated that social and emotional learning incorporates direct and indirect instruction into all areas of life. Students learn social and emotional intelligence by examples, experience, and reflection.

Attitude and professionalism in how students are treated set a powerful example. Professors may use problems and conflicts that arise to engage students to be responsive, reflective, nonviolent, and creative. Their treatment of students with interest, respect, courtesy, and kindness creates a culture of acceptance and respect for all students. Letting the students know that this was done deliberately and with effort can be a learning opportunity. Thus, professors provide the modeling needed to learn vicariously

Table 4.1. Suggested Questions for Developing Students' Awareness and Constructive Thinking

1. Have you experienced a situation like this?
2. Have you ever been forced to make a decision or solve a problem when you were upset or angry?
3. Have you ever changed your feelings by changing your thoughts about the event?
4. When you were in a particular situation, did you think of the consequences?
5. Do you make demands or express preferences?
6. Have you ever challenged your own irrational beliefs?
7. Do you feel better knowing that, even though you can't control everything about a problem, you can control some things?
8. When you have had a serious problem without an immediate solution, how have you coped until the problem was worked out?
9. Have you identified the short-term goals to help you achieve the long-term goals?
10. How do you affect your relationships with your family, friends, and colleagues?
11. What can you do if you don't value something others value?
12. What is it like for you to receive criticism? How do you feel? What do you say to yourself?
13. What does it mean for you to succeed or fail?
14. How would you describe reasonable or unreasonable reactions to emotions?
15. Are you aware of your moods?
16. How do you deal with worry, fear, anxiety, shame, and guilt?
17. Do you challenge your irrational beliefs during intense emotions?

(Bandura 1996). Any emotional intelligence coaching or mentoring will be futile if the actions are contrary to what is taught.

In higher education, emotional intelligence need not be a particular program or method. In fact, it may limit the delivery options to certain themes or designs, which may not meet the professor's needs. Additional instruction on emotional intelligence may not fit the curriculum schedule, and it can get costly to hire someone to add the curriculum. The professor's awareness of the opportunities to make connections between emotional intelligence and the content provides a way to transition into class discussion about relational topics. By asking the right kinds of questions, students' awareness and constructive thinking may be increased. The questions listed in Table 4.1 are just samples and are not intended to be exhaustive.

Pasi (2001) suggested that emotional intelligence mentoring and coaching be infused in the content being taught. Consider the curriculum that will provide opportunities for students to learn problem-solving, decision-making, and analysis skills. Counseling class is the best place to start because discussions about human behaviors are the main topic. What emotional intelligence skills are needed to improve human dilemmas? As students monitor their own progress and set personal goals, they will be more aware of their responsibility in the process. Humanities and social

NEW DIRECTIONS FOR TEACHING AND LEARNING • DOI: 10.1002/tl

sciences provide vast opportunities to gain multiple perspectives on events that have led to national and global problems. Students can learn about themselves in relation to others in the historical perspectives.

Analysis of the social cognitive learning can take various forms. Professors can choose from a variety of methods, such as group discussions and debates, script writing and role-playing, reflection and journal writing, use of artistic expression, and reaction to media and other presentations (Pasi 2001). Students in higher education are more capable of expression and communication. Yet communication skills seem to be hit or miss for many people because they are not explicitly taught. Egan (2010) pointed out that even though communication skills are needed for everyday interaction, most people are not equipped with such skills, which can be the basis for interpersonal difficulties. The hope for emotional intelligence training is to have communication skills be explicitly taught and practiced. Instead of making judgments, being critical, or blaming, people can learn to rephrase, ask for clarification, check for accuracy, make a statement about their understanding, and wait for feedback. The ability to take the perspective of others is an indication of higher emotional intelligence.

Communication skills are crucial to the success of mentorship or coaching. The helpers need to attend to the conversation, listen actively, assist the student to stay focused, and challenge misperceptions. Turn taking, connecting, and mutual influence are in every conversation (Egan 2010). Most educational professionals and professors are equipped to be mentors or coaches to promote emotional intelligence. Within the context of their core subject, opportunities arise for social and emotional intelligence learning. The priority to infuse emotional intelligence must be communicated to students. As more professors take up the challenge, the culture of education can change to promote emotional intelligence, whereby a group serves as agents of change (Bandura 2002).

The urgency of promoting emotional intelligence in higher education in Asian universities can be explained in terms of economics. As Asian industries and companies develop and take center stage, there is more need for people with emotional intelligence in leadership positions. Higher education in Asia is a place to promote emotional intelligence in students so that the vicious cycle that maintains ill effects of low emotional intelligence can be broken. The modern world has changed, and it is no longer about domination but collaboration. As we saw in the global economic collapse in 2008, nations are interlinked. Failure in one nation can have a ripple effect on others. People need to work together, solve world problems, and share the resources. While the high priority on educational achievement in Asia is well known, equally important is the high priority on emotional intelligence.

Academic achievement is not enough to sustain success when interpersonal and intrapersonal skills found in emotional intelligence are not developed (Goleman 1995). The high number of Asian students who have gone to top colleges has not translated to a similar proportion of Asian students in leadership positions. The "glass ceiling" describes the limitation of Asians in leadership roles (Varma 2004). Regardless of the level of achievement, if emotional intelligence is ignored, the long-term effect may be the "glass ceiling" among Asians across the globe.

Conclusion

The world is getting smaller as people travel across continents to seek opportunities. Even though the cultural differences seem obvious, emotional intelligence is relevant across cultures because the human brain operates in the same way to make sense of the emotional information. The cultural beliefs and values are generally perpetuated even when they are no longer valid. Without education and awareness, change may not be possible. It is no longer the cultural beliefs that determine how people function but the financial competition that drives the modern world. Across the globe, cities are developing and technology is advancing. Families have to work extra hard to make ends meet in Asia. As a result, children's emotional well-being has been neglected, and these children go on to become students in higher education. For this reason, educational systems must include social and emotional intelligence learning. Higher education in Asia is the best place to promote emotional intelligence because society is more global than ever before, with leaders and professionals working throughout the world. The traditional education in Asia has focused on academic achievement and test scores. The educational systems are generally hierarchical, where students are expected to listen and follow directions. Memorization is a primary method of learning. Emotional awareness, constructive thinking, and problem solving are not modeled. As a result, young people become adults with low emotional intelligence. They are not ready to meet the challenges of the twenty-first century.

Emotional intelligence coaching and mentoring in higher education offer hope for leadership, problem solving, and effective communication by fostering empathy, social responsibility, and interpersonal skills. Young people in higher education today are capable of improving the future direction when emotional intelligence is promoted. Instead of competition and self-interest, imagine a world where all people are valued for their talents and skills because their high emotional intelligence has allowed them to function to their highest potential and to self-actualize. Instead of winners and losers, people can look toward global citizenship where they share the common goal to improve human conditions and everyone contributes to the functioning of society within a continuum of abilities. As Asian students become professionals who can communicate effectively, solve problems, lead, and share social responsibility, the world can rely on Asian leaders and professionals. Emotional intelligence is what brings people together to be better human beings and to have a positive impact on people in the immediate environment and beyond.

References

Bachorowski, J., and M. J. Owren. 2002. "Vocal Acoustics in Emotional Intelligence." In *The Wisdom in Feeling: Psychological Processes in Emotional Intelligence*, edited by L. F. Barrett and P. Salovey, 11–36. New York: Guilford Press.

Bandura, A. 1996. "Ontological and Epistemological Terrains Revisited." *Journal of Behavior Therapy and Experimental Psychiatry* 27:323–345.

Bandura, A. 2002. "Social Cognitive Theory in Cultural Context." *Applied Psychology: An International Review* 51:269–290.

Banks, J. A. 2008. "Diversity, Group Identity, and Citizenship Education in a Global Age." *Educational Researcher* 37:129–139.

Bar-On, R. 2001. "Emotional Intelligence and Self-Actualization." In *Emotional Intelligence in Everyday Life: A Scientific Inquiry*, edited by J. Ciarrochi, J. P. Forgas, and J. D. Mayer, 82–97. Philadelphia: Psychology Press.

Bar-On, R. 2004. *Bar-On Emotional Quotient Inventory*. New York: Multi-Health Systems.

Bar-On, R., and J. D. Parker, eds. 2002. *The Handbook of Emotional Intelligence*. San Francisco: Jossey-Bass.

Barrett, L. F., and P. Salovey, eds. 2002. *The Wisdom in Feeling: Psychological Processes in Emotional Intelligence*. New York: Guilford Press.

Berthrong, J. H., and E. N. Berthrong. 2000. *Confucianism: A Short Introduction*. Oxford, England: Oneworld Publications.

Bond, M. H. 1987. *The Psychology of the Chinese People*. New York: Oxford University Press.

Bradley, J. 2012, August. *School-Based Family Counseling and World Peace*. Paper presented at the Oxford Symposium for School Based Family Counseling, Brasenose College, Oxford University, England.

Ciarrochi, J., F. P. Deane, and C. J. Wilson. 2002. "Adolescents Who Need Help Most Are the Least Likely to Seek It: The Relationship between Low Emotional Competence and Low Intention to Seek Help." *British Journal of Guidance and Counselling* 30:173–188.

Dweck, C. S. 1988. "A Social Cognition Approach to Learning." *Psychology Review* 95:256–273.

Egan, G. 2010. *The Skilled Helper: A Problem-Management and Opportunity-Development Approach to Helping*. Belmont, CA: Brooks/Cole, Cengage Learning.

Elfenbein, H. A., A. A. Marsh, and N. Ambady. 2002. "Emotional Intelligence and the Recognition of Emotion from Facial Expressions." In *The Wisdom in Feeling: Psychological Processes in Emotional Intelligence*, edited by L. F. Barrett and P. Salovey, 37–59. New York: Guilford Press.

Epstein, S. 1998. *Constructive Thinking: The Key to Emotional Intelligence*. Westport, CT: Praeger.

Forgas, J. P. 2001. *Handbook of Affect and Social Cognition*. Mahwah, NJ: Lawrence Erlbaum Associates.

Fung, H., and E. C. Chen. 2001. "Across Time and beyond Skin: Self and Transgression in the Everyday Socialization of Shame among Taiwanese Preschool Children." *Social Development* 10:420–437.

Fung, H., E. Lieber, and P. W. Leung. 2003. "Parental Beliefs about Shame and Moral Socialization in Taiwan, Hong Kong and the United States." In *Progress in Asian Social Psychology: Conceptual and Empirical Contributions*, edited by G. Yang, K. Hwang, P. B. Pederson, and I. Daibo, 78–106. Westport, CT: Praeger.

Gardner, H. 1993. *Frames of Mind: The Theory of Multiple Intelligences*. New York: Basic Books.

Gohm, C. L., and G. L. Clore. 2002. "Affect as Information: An Individual-Differences Approach." In *The Wisdom in Feeling: Psychological Processes in Emotional Intelligence*, edited by L. F. Barrett and P. Salovey, 89–113. New York: Guilford Press.

Goleman, D. 1995. *Emotional Intelligence*. New York: Bantam Books.

Goleman, D. 1998. *Working with Emotional Intelligence*. New York: Bantam Books.

Goleman, D., R. Boyatzis, and A. McKee. 2002. *Primal Leadership: Realizing the Power of Emotional Intelligence*. Boston: Harvard Business School Press.

Ho, D. Y.-F., W. Fu, and S. M. Ng. 2004. "Guilt, Shame and Embarrassment: Revelations of Face and Self." *Culture and Psychology* 10:64–84.

Jennings, C. M., and X. Di. 1996. "Collaborative Learning and Thinking: The Vygotskian Approach." In *Vygotsky in the Classroom: Mediated Literacy Instruction and Assessment*, edited by L. Dixon-Krauss, 77–91. White Plains, NY: Longman.

Kelly, G. A. 1955. *A Theory of Personality: The Psychology of Personal Constructs*. New York: W.W. Norton.

Kember, D., C. Hong, and A. Ho. 2008. "Characterizing the Motivational Orientation of Students in Higher Education: A Naturalistic Study in Three Hong Kong Universities." *British Journal of Educational Psychology* 78:313–329.

Kozulin, A. 2004. "Vygotsky's Theory in the Classroom: Introduction." *European Journal of Psychology of Education* 19:3–7.

Lau, A. S., N. M. Jernewall, N. Zane, and H. F. Myers. 2002. "Correlates of Suicidal Behaviors among Asian American Outpatient Youths." *Cultural Diversity and Ethnic Minority Psychology* 8:199–213.

LeDoux, J. E. 1996. *The Emotional Brain: The Mysterious Underpinnings of Emotional Life*. New York: Simon & Schuster.

Lee, K. H. 1999. "Korean American Preschoolers' Motivational Helplessness and Its Association with Beliefs about Goodness/Badness." *Journal of Research in Childhood Education* 14:103–117.

Leung, F. K. S. 2001. "In Search of an East Asian Identity in Mathematics Education." *Educational Studies in Mathematics* 47:35–51.

Lewkowicz, A. 1999. *Teaching Emotional Intelligence: Making Informed Choices*. Arlington Heights, IL: Skylight Professional Development.

Maté, G. 1999. *Scattered*. New York: Penguin Putnam.

Matsumoto, D., ed. 1997. *Culture and Modern Life*. Pacific Grove, CA: Brooks/Cole.

Mayer, J. D. 2001. "A Field Guide to Emotional Intelligence." In *Emotional Intelligence in Everyday Life: A Scientific Inquiry*, edited by J. Ciarrochi, J. P. Forgas, and J. D. Mayer, 3–24. Philadelphia: Psychology Press.

Mischel, W., Y. Shoda, and O. Ayduk. 2008. *Introduction to Personality: Toward an Integrative Science of the Person*, 8th ed. Hoboken, NJ: John Wiley & Sons.

Moore, B. 2009. "Emotional Intelligence for School Administrators: A Priority for School Reform?" *American Secondary Education* 37:20–28.

Neville, H. J., and J. T. Bruer. 2001. "Language Processing: How Experience Affects Brain Organization." In *Critical Thinking about Critical Periods*, edited by D. B. Bailey Jr., J. T. Bruer, F. J. Symons, and J. W. Lichtman, 151–172. Baltimore, MD: Paul H. Brookes.

O'Connor, E., and K. McCartney. 2007. "Examining Teacher–Child Relationships and Achievement as Part of an Ecological Model of Development." *American Educational Research Journal* 44:340–369.

Pasi, R. J. 2001. *High Expectations: Promoting Social Emotional Learning and Academic Achievement in Your School*. New York: Teachers College, Columbia University.

Rogers, C. R. 1961. *On Becoming a Person*, 2nd ed. Boston: Houghton Mifflin.

Saarni, C. 2000. "Emotional Competence: A Developmental Perspective." In *The Handbook of Emotional Intelligence*, edited by R. Bar-On and J. D. Parker, 68–91. San Francisco: Jossey-Bass.

Salovey, P. 2001. "Applied Emotional Intelligence: Regulating Emotions to Become Healthy, Wealthy and Wise." In *Emotional Intelligence in Everyday Life: A Scientific Inquiry*, edited by J. Ciarrochi, J. P. Forgas, and J. D. Mayer, 168–184. Philadelphia: Psychology Press.

Salovey, P., and J. D. Mayer. 1990. "Emotional Intelligence." *Imagination, Cognition, and Personality* 9:185–211.

Song, Y. 2002. "Crisis of Cultural Identity in East Asia: On the Meaning of Confucian Ethics in the Age of Globalization." *Asian Philosophy* 12:109–125.

Stewart, V. 2007. *Becoming Citizens of the World: The Best of Educational Leadership 2006–2007*. Alexandria, VA: Association for Supervision and Curriculum Development.

Sung, H. Y. 2010. "The Influence of Culture on Parenting Practices of East Asian Families and Emotional Intelligence of Older Adolescents: A Qualitative Study." *School Psychology International* 31:199–214.

Sung, H. Y. 2013. *From Adult to Children: Creating a Culture That Promotes EiQ*. Cupertino, CA: CreateSpace, an Amazon Company (self-published).

Taylor, G. J. 2001. "Low Emotional Intelligence and Mental Illness." In *Emotional Intelligence in Everyday Life: A Scientific Inquiry*, edited by J. Ciarrochi, J. P. Forgas, and J. D. Mayer, 76–81. Philadelphia: Psychology Press.

Thorndike, E. L. 1905. *The Elements of Psychology*. New York: A.G. Seiler.

Vandervoort, D. J. 2006. "The Importance of Emotional Intelligence in Higher Education." *Current Psychology: Developmental, Learning, Personality, Social* 25:4–7.

Varma, R. 2004. "Asian Americans: Achievements Mask Challenges." *Asian Journal of Social Science* 32:290–307.

Vernon, A. 1989. *Thinking, Feeling, Behaving: An Emotional Education Curriculum for Adolescents*. Champaign, IL: Research Press.

Wang, L. 2006. "Sociocultural Learning Theories and Information Literacy Teaching Activities in Higher Education." *Reference and User Services Quarterly* 47:149–158.

Yang, S., and P. C. Rosenblatt. 2001. "Shame in Korean Families." *Journal of Comparative Family Studies* 32:361–375.

Yeh, K. 2003. "The Beneficial and Harmful Effects of Filial Piety: An Integrative Analysis." In *Progress in Asian Social Psychology: Conceptual and Empirical Contributions*, edited by G. Yang, K. Hwang, P. B. Pederson, and I. Daibo, 67–82. Westport, CT: Praeger.

HELEN Y. SUNG is a school psychologist and adjunct professor in the Department of Education on the San Jose campus of the University of San Francisco.

This chapter examines the use of reading and writing activities to promote critical reflection among Asian students in higher education settings.

Reading and Writing for Critical Reflective Thinking

Mary M. Chittooran

Embedded in constructivist approaches to teaching and learning, collaborative knowledge construction is characterized by the creation of shared meaning (Woolfolk 2013), a concept that makes particular sense during reading and writing given the cognitive demands and subjective interpretations of content that are associated with such activities. Instructors in higher education settings can harness the potential of reading and writing activities to facilitate critical reflective thinking in their students that can contribute to collaborative knowledge construction. This chapter provides an introduction to critical reflection, discusses ways to promote critical reflective thinking among students in Asian and non-Asian contexts, and, finally, offers a number of reading and writing activities that utilize and enhance critical reflection.

Before we go further, it is important to point out that while this chapter focuses on Asian students, it may also be applied—with some modification—to *all* students in higher education. Additionally, because the academic and social-behavioral characteristics of Asian students are addressed in the first volume of this two-volume series (Guo 2015; van Schalkwyk 2015), this chapter will not risk redundancy by addressing those in detail. However, very briefly, teaching and learning among Asians, particularly those of Chinese origin, are based on the traditional Confucian approach, which is characterized by unidirectional delivery of information from instructor to student, academic rigor, and rote memorization rather than active engagement with and transformation of the material to be learned. Knowledge is perceived as simple and certain rather than complex and uncertain (Qian and Pan 2002; Schommer-Aikins and Easter 2008).

Given that Asian students come from a culture with a centuries-old emphasis on traditional approaches to behaving, teaching, and learning (Xu et al. 2005; Yong et al. 2010), it is clear that a paradigmatic shift to

New Directions for Teaching and Learning, no. 143, Fall 2015 © 2015 Wiley Periodicals, Inc.
Published online in Wiley Online Library (wileyonlinelibrary.com) • DOI: 10.1002/tl.20137

thinking differently about how we access, engage with, and use knowledge is not without its challenges and may indeed encounter resistance. However, the potential rewards associated with such a change include stronger interpersonal connections, improved communication, more effective problem solving, and, ultimately, enhanced learning. In addition, such an approach may empower Asian students by giving them the tools they need to compete in the global arena.

Critical Reflective Thinking

Although John Dewey (1933) is generally credited with originating the concept of reflection, he actually drew on the ideas of pioneering thinkers such as Aristotle, Plato, and Confucius. Reflection involves examining and making connections among our experiences in order to promote increasingly complex and interrelated mental schema. This examination of commonalities, interrelationships, differences, and aberrations can result in problem solution and the development of higher-order thinking skills. Dewey observed that reflective thinking is called for when individuals recognize that some problems cannot be solved with certainty; that is, there are some problems for which there are no yes or no answers. Although some authors use the terms *critical reflection* and *critical reflective thinking* interchangeably with *reflective thinking*, and others use the term simply to address in-depth, evaluative reflection, this chapter will use Hatton and Smith's (1995, 45) definition, which states that critical reflective thinking involves the process of analyzing, reconsidering, and questioning experiences within a broader context of issues that are influenced by prevailing "social, political, and/or cultural forces." The purpose of critical reflection is to challenge our own assumptions and to arrive at a deeper, more complex understanding of a phenomenon; in that sense, critical reflection is transformational in nature (Brookfield 1995; Mezirow 1990). For example, Shadiow (2013) reported that college faculty who reconceptualize, examine, and interpret their own stories within a critical incidents framework not only develop a deeper understanding of teaching, but also become more effective teachers.

According to Brookfield (1995) and Mezirow (1998), critical reflection involves four features. The first, *assumption analysis*, involves becoming aware of our assumptions and their impact on our daily activities as well as a willingness to temporarily suspend those assumptions. *Contextual awareness* has to do with our recognition that our assumptions are created within and are unique to our own cultural and historical contexts. *Imaginative speculation* allows individuals to develop alternative explanations for commonly held knowledge, and *reflective skepticism* represents the culmination of the first three activities and involves questioning "universal truth claims or unexamined patterns of interaction" outside the context in which they are usually examined.

NEW DIRECTIONS FOR TEACHING AND LEARNING • DOI: 10.1002/tl

Promoting Critical Reflection in the Asian Classroom

Many instructors in higher education recognize that developing reflective abilities in their students is an important responsibility. In teacher preparation programs in the United States, for example, the development of reflective practitioners—those who not only are technically competent teachers but who also actively seek to improve their practice through an ongoing, dynamic process of reflection on their teaching—is often a clearly stated goal that drives instruction. Given this, it clearly falls on the shoulders of instructors to help develop reflective thinkers in their classrooms. This can be accomplished through all phases of the teaching and learning process: planning and implementation of instruction, formative and summative assessment, and providing feedback to students.

Critical reflection ought to be a built-in goal for every higher education curriculum, both in Asian and in non-Asian contexts. It should be intentionally included on every syllabus and every plan for study, and course objectives should address how the course will incorporate activities that promote critical reflection, with the appropriate modifications for students with disabilities. Instructional efforts should be aimed at modeling, teaching, providing opportunities for, practicing, and reinforcing such reflection. Formative assessments, which are dynamic, ongoing assessments that tell instructors and students how well the instructional process is going, can provide opportunities for critical reflection. For example, some quick formative assessments might include in-class writing prompts such as "Describe one thing you learned today that challenged you to think differently about what you already know." Summative assessments, which are final, end-of-unit or end-of-instruction assessments that tell us about the success of instructional outcomes, could include term papers, final exams, and individual or group projects. These could incorporate a section on reflection; for example, students who have developed their own code of ethics in an applied ethics course could reflect on their thought processes or reasons for inclusion of various elements, or could be asked to provide justification for how their own values align with their code. Finally, feedback provided by instructors to students during and after instruction can be designed to encourage students to engage in reflection about what they have learned and what they might still learn, and to think about the material in a deeper way.

Collaboration with peers has been found to promote critical reflection among college students. While such learning is not typical in most Asian settings, instructors in these classrooms can provide opportunities for collaborative learning. Hatton and Smith (1995) examined students in a four-year secondary education program who were assigned to critical friends dyads in which they completed peer interviews, wrote reports, and reflected on factors that had influenced their professional choices. Results found that engagement with another person in a safe setting that encouraged honest dialogue, questioning, confronting, and challenging promoted active reflection in a way that other activities did not. The authors speculated that students engaged in deeper reflection when they were given opportunities to distance themselves from their own actions and ideas and hold them up for scrutiny in front of a trusted, nonjudgmental peer. Regardless of the subject matter, students working in small groups tend to learn more of what is taught and to retain it longer than when the same content is presented in other instructional formats. Other research studies (Hatton and Smith 1995; Mayer 2008; Tsay and Brady 2010) show that collaborative learning opportunities have helped students demonstrate improvements in academic achievement and test scores, higher-level thinking skills, creative functioning, and critical thinking. In addition, students who work in collaborative groups also report being more satisfied with their classes and with their performance in those classes.

There are several instructional approaches designed to encourage critical reflection in both Asian and non-Asian contexts. *Questioning* can be a powerful tool to promote reflection in the classroom (Woolfolk 2013). Questions may be of the closed type (those that can be answered with a simple yes or no) or the open-ended type (those without a clear, dichotomous answer or those that are likely to engender a variety of responses). Generally, closed questions are less likely to result in reflection than are open-ended ones. For example, instead of asking, "Have you thought about obstacles to the proposed intervention?" (a question that could simply be answered in the affirmative or the negative), one could ask, "What kinds of obstacles do you anticipate with the proposed intervention?" or even better, because it is more open-ended, "What factors might have an impact on the success of the proposed intervention?" In addition, students who read a passage could develop a list of questions to be used as a reading guide. To make the task more challenging and to require them to use their reflective thinking skills, students could be asked to come up with a variety of fact-based, interpretative, or evaluative kinds of questions. Students could also be asked to develop test questions that incorporate a reflective component, and instructors could then include one or more of those questions in tests and exams.

Although questioning can be a useful approach to promoting reflection, the questions have to be the right kind of questions. For example, factual questions do not promote reflection ("What are the four functions of a theory?"), nor do questions that simply pose hypothetical situations, however intriguing they might be ("Imagine that you are stranded on a desert island. What four items do you wish you had with you?"). On the other hand, prompts that require students to delve deeply into themselves are more likely to promote critical reflection ("Imagine that you are writing a letter to your 15-year-old self. What lessons have you learned that would help your teenage self to navigate the coming years most successfully?").

Questions designed to promote reflection can be used between teachers and students as well as between students and their peers. When used between teachers and students, they can be used as part of instruction but may also be used when providing feedback to students on assignments or exams. Students who ask questions about challenging reading material may find themselves critically reflecting on those readings and trying to make sense of them. Students in study groups who work on making meaning of material together are more likely to engage in critical reflection if they ask themselves questions that toggle their own conceptual analyses of course concepts, instead of factual questions that require simple recognition or recall.

The kind of *feedback* typically provided in most college classrooms does not promote reflection in students. However, instructors who employ evaluative kinds of feedback such that the learner continues to think about the topic in different ways may be able to promote reflection. For example, in a course on secondary methods of teaching English, a comment conducive to reflection would be: "Good discussion of alternative approaches to teaching this concept. How will you relate your approach to Jay's unique interests?" Instructors may point out other possibilities that help students think about interrelationships among factors that have not previously been considered: "This token economy you've described works well with older elementary school students. How do you think it might work with Susan, given that she's an adolescent? Might it be more effective? Less effective?" Feedback is often provided in writing, but is probably most useful when instructors and students also meet for a face-to-face conversation that will allow for direct communication and perception checking.

Another possibility for encouraging critical reflection may include *seeking alternative explanations* and asking students to engage in perspective taking—that is, to put themselves in the shoes of another person ("Think about how the Native Americans might have experienced Christopher Columbus's arrival in the New World"), asking students to provide a theoretical framework for a dissertation, comparing and contrasting one or more pedagogical approaches, and asking them to place themselves in varied contexts ("Imagine that you are an adolescent living in the early fifteenth century. What challenges might you experience that you would not experience today?"). Asking "What if?" questions also encourages reflection; for example, students in an English literature class might be asked to respond to a prompt such as "There is some controversy about whether William Shakespeare actually wrote his plays. What if he had *not* written them? What are the implications?" Students working on group projects could be asked, "How might your work—the process, the product, or both—have been different if you had *not* been on the team?" rather than "What did you bring to the team?" Students can also be asked to consider the consequences of their choices. In a professional ethics class, students who find a solution to a moral dilemma can be asked to reflect on their solution, and to consider their decision-making process as well as the consequences—both anticipated and unintended—of their decision.

Research has also shown that *writing in journals* can promote reflection among college students. Hatton and Smith (1995) examined the efficacy of using social interaction among students in combination with their journal writing experiences to increase both the quality and quantity of reflective thinking. They examined four kinds of writing—technical, descriptive, dialogic reflection, and critical reflection—and found that critical reflection was enhanced by the use of journal writing, especially when the entries were shared with class listservs.

Kaplan, Rupley, Sparks, and Holcomb (2007) compared preservice teachers' use of individual journals with journals that were shared online with classmates, and found that the latter were significantly more likely to contain evidence of reflective thinking than the former and that entries could be categorized into one of the four types of reflection described by Hatton and Smith (1995). Short and Rinehart (1991) reported on an effort to use journals to promote critical reflective thinking in a small sample of 10 students in educational administration doctoral cohorts. Basing their efforts partly on Donald Schon's work on reflective practitioners, the authors developed a critical reflection model they used with their students. Journals were completed by students over the course of a year and were designed to help students become more reflective, prepare to face complex and multilayered problems in their future work settings, and take on the identity of school principals. Journal entries were coded in seven categories, ranging from "No descriptive language" to "Explanation with consideration of moral, ethical, political issues." Results found that most students evidenced an increase in level of reflection over the course of the study and that there were significant improvements in both the quantity and the quality of journal entries.

The research literature offers some evidence that efforts to promote reflection have been successful. For example, Griffin (2003) used critical incidents with preservice teachers and found that such writing increased the students' orientation toward growth and inquiry. Self-assessments completed by the students showed an emergence of qualities of open-mindedness, responsibility, and wholeheartedness, characteristics that Dewey attributed to reflective individuals.

Challenges in Promoting Critical Reflection

There is not a great deal of research evidence that supports the successful use of critical reflection in higher education. Many instructors seem to view critical reflection as a desirable goal for the classroom but do not implement it for one reason or another. Griffin (2003) observed, surveyed, and interviewed instructors regarding their perceptions of the impact of group learning on academic achievement, and while most respondents (85 percent) saw discussion as the best way to develop critical thinking and acknowledged that developing critical thinking was an important goal, it was also apparent that despite some isolated efforts at small group work and activities, many instructors fell back on traditional instructional approaches.

NEW DIRECTIONS FOR TEACHING AND LEARNING • DOI: 10.1002/tl

Gustafson and Bennett (2002) found that trying to promote reflection among military cadets through the use of diaries generally did not produce responses indicating deep reflection. In their work, they identified 11 variables that affected the cadets' lack of reflective behavior. These 11 variables were organized into three main groups: the first group included *student variables* such as skill and experience in reflective thinking, motivation, mental set, and comfort with the purpose and process of reflection. The second group, *environmental variables*, included a physical environment that was conducive to reflection as well as an interpersonal environment where cadets felt emotionally safe engaging in reflection. The final group of variables had to do with the *reflection task* itself. These included the nature of the prompts for reflection, elaboration, and contemplation (the more demanding the prompts, the more likely students were to respond); the format in which reflections were to be presented (written formats were more effective than oral ones); the kind of feedback following the prompts; and the instructional and behavioral consequences of reflection. Of all those variables, the authors concluded that manipulations of the interpersonal environment held the most promise for encouraging reflection.

Hatton and Smith (1995) have cited the following reasons for the difficulty in promoting reflection: a lack of time and opportunity for reflection, pedagogical unpreparedness for promoting reflective thinking, an inability to apply reflective thinking to real-life situations, and the shame associated with revealing vulnerability or one's private thoughts. It also may be that the relative newness of critical reflection as an instructional approach, fear of change, an unwillingness to give up control in the classroom, or simply poor fit for the individual instructor could pose challenges in implementation. Asian students and their instructors may find these challenges compounded by cultural factors that impinge on the teaching and learning process.

Despite these difficulties, critical reflective thinking in the college classroom is not only a worthwhile goal but a practice that is beneficial to both students and teachers. Hatton and Smith (1995) recommend using social interaction to facilitate reflection in that it stimulates students' abilities to think, clarify, and critique pedagogical ideas and practice. It also offers a safe, nonthreatening space to reveal vulnerability. Some other approaches that might be useful are encouraging dialogue among students, providing probes ("Clarify what you meant when you said ... "), and asking for alternative interpretations ("What other explanations might there be for Richard's actions?").

Reading and Writing Activities to Promote Critical Reflection in the Asian Classroom

The following section of this chapter addresses the use of reading and writing activities to promote critical reflection for collaborative knowledge construction, both in Asian and in non-Asian contexts. Some of the techniques emphasize reading and discussion, others emphasize writing and discussion, and still others focus on both reading and writing. Generally, though, all of them require students to critically reflect on material and then work collaboratively with their peers to construct knowledge. Suggestions have been culled from the work of Driscoll (2009), Lyman (1981), Hatton and Smith (1995), Woolfolk (2013), Ormrod (2011, 2013), the University of Texas Center for Teaching and Learning (n.d.), and the instructional experiences of this author. It is important to note that while all of these approaches may utilize the traditional pen-and-paper method, they all lend themselves to electronic use as well. In fact, writing, spelling, grammar usage, self-checking, and self-correcting are simplified with word processing programs, especially for speakers of other languages.

Structured Curriculum Tasks.   Structured curriculum tasks have the broadest application, as they can be used in almost any setting, with any subject matter, and with any group of students; in fact, their use is limited only by the creativity of the instructor. The goal of instructors who want to utilize the existing curriculum is to integrate reading and writing activities with critical reflection as much as possible. For example, in an English class, the instructor may ask students to read nonfiction excerpts independently, and then come together in a group to discuss and make meaning of them. In an introductory qualitative research course, the use of an observation protocol can be used to teach about qualitative methodologies. Students can observe children in a school setting, and can then collaboratively compare and make meaning of their findings. In field-based courses such as a school psychology practicum, student teams can be taught to integrate interview information with other data about the client, collaboratively practice looking for patterns, and have a mock assessment team meeting where they present their findings and diagnostic impressions. Graduate or undergraduate students in a clinical assessment class may be assigned a client and then work collaboratively on the assessment. One student could do classroom observations, another could meet with parents, a third could conduct a clinical interview with the child, yet another could be responsible for psychological testing, and a fifth could assess academic achievement. Students would be responsible for providing a report on their own assessment activities and then individually reflecting on the findings. Once they had come up with initial impressions, they would present the case to the others and then together reflect on and critically evaluate the child's functioning and recommend next steps. Report writing could also be a collaborative activity.

In a graduate course in life span development, students might be asked to identify a child to observe and then interview the child's family and teachers about a specific observed behavior. They could be asked to do background reading on the child, complete a comprehensive literature review on the particular behavioral issue, share their findings with their classmates,

_..en use group critical reflection to come up with a diagnostic summary and recommendations.

Other curriculum activities that use reading and writing require students to complete narratives, biographies, and reflective essays. In each of these cases, the writing process could be made a reflective one by having students submit the work, receive instructor or peer feedback, and then work to improve the quality of their submission.

Journal Writing. Journal writing may range from jotting down random thoughts about an event or a reading assignment to systematically recording daily, weekly, or monthly entries on a topic of interest. Journals usually involve a more informal style of writing, without the strict adherence to grammar rules that would normally be expected in more formal writing. Journals can be of the conventional paper-and-pen type or, increasingly, can be completed on a laptop, smartphone, or iPad. Journals may be shared with small groups or the whole class, may be submitted to the instructor for periodic checking or grading, or may simply be kept to oneself and be used as a way to promote private reflection. Journal writing can support critical reflective thinking, and, because of its intentional nature, can also enhance observational skills and short- and long-term memory function. Further, journal writing can promote cognitive functioning or, more specifically, declarative ("know that"), procedural ("know how"), and conditional ("know when") knowledge (Woolfolk 2013).

Journal writing can also be used to help with *mentor-guided reflections* on a critical incident. Students can either write about something significant that happened to them or be asked to react to a critical incident provided by the instructor. Another commonly used technique involves students being asked to keep a reading journal. Journal writing for critical reflection and collaborative knowledge construction can be useful if a purpose and guidelines for writing are provided for students; if not, journaling becomes a purposeless activity that lacks utility as a learning technique.

Double-entry journal writing is a form of journaling that can be completed individually or collaboratively, and helps students read material critically, develop questions about the material, and share it with others. Students typically use a large hardcover journal and divide each page vertically into two sides. On the left side, they enter key points or concepts; on the right, they jot down responses to the key points, questions that may arise, or critical reflections. They may share these with their peers, use the entries to start a discussion, or complete a paired annotation (see next section). The advantage of a double-entry journal is that its format requires readers to slow down and think about what they are reading. It promises to be a particularly useful technique for Asian students who may struggle with the English language, may want to note thoughts for a later time, or may need to seek feedback from their peers.

Writing Groups. A writing group is characterized as a group of individuals, ideally three to five, who come together for the express purpose of working on their writing in a collaborative setting. While such groups typically function in an informal setting, there is no reason that they cannot be equally effective in a more formal setting such as the college classroom. Writing group members may be self-selected or may be assigned to writing groups based on their instructor's judgment. Writing groups may be most useful for improving student writing, getting feedback on one's ongoing writing efforts, reflecting on one's own and others' writing, and collaboratively improving both the process and the product of writing. Writing groups may be particularly useful when instructors are able to pair native speakers of English with nonnative speakers; such combinations help both groups of students academically, in addition to enhancing interpersonal interactions.

Students also pair up to read, review, or learn the main concepts of a journal article or an assigned reading and then provide a summary of the reading. *Paired annotations* can be used in most subject areas but may be most effective in the liberal arts. Students then use double-entry journals to discuss key points and to look for similarities and differences in their analyses. Students could also prepare a composite annotation that summarizes the reading and provides a full bibliographic citation. If these annotations are completed around a particular topic, they may be easily shared with other students working on their own topics. For example, a group of students collaborating on a paper could break up the literature review into its component parts and then provide paired annotations on their particular topic.

Action Research Projects.   An action research project, particularly if it is collaborative and intended for joint presentation and publication, can be a fruitful source of learning in a qualitative research course. Students can collaboratively decide on a topic after having read the background literature, can work to narrow the topic, and then can conduct research, perhaps taking on various roles as necessary. One student could be responsible for the literature review, another for developing an interview protocol, and yet another for completing the observations. Once the data have been gathered, the group can come together to analyze and then write up the data for presentation or publication. It would probably be at this stage that the project would call for the deepest reflection when students work together to make sense of the data, develop themes, and decide what to report and how to report it.

Case Studies.   A case is a narrated account of a real-world situation or a teacher-constructed situation that simulates real life and that sets up a problem for students to solve. Case studies can be used with small groups of students to stimulate critical reflection and to promote collaborative knowledge construction in the higher education classroom. Instructors might structure classroom procedures so that students are each given the case, are asked to read it fully, and then come to class to find a solution to the case. Since each student will bring his or her own orientation and background

he solutions they come up with will inevitably
be used for group work, so that students can
ysis to other group members and critically re-
tions. Students can then collaboratively work

ng.   Problem-based learning (PBL) is a col-
that had its inception in medical education
...creasingly being used in the liberal arts arena
as well. Students are given information about real-world, complex, usually multilayered problems that require solution. Problems are most often worked on collaboratively; however, they also lend themselves to individual solution. The advantage of this approach is that it can be used to
encourage teamwork, communication, and problem-solving skills in students. The instructor's role changes from being a lecturer to being a resource person, coach, and facilitator of problem solving. Depending on the
instructor, the students, and the subject, this approach holds a great deal of
promise for critical reflection and collaborative knowledge construction. It
also has the potential for being used in a variety of settings with a variety of
subjects.

For example, in a graduate applied ethics course cotaught by the author (Chittooran 2014), which drew students from public health, law, public policy, and education, students were directed to a low-income, urban
neighborhood that was once flourishing but had since fallen into disrepair.
The students' task was to generate one or more solutions that would revi-
talize this once-grand community. Working in multidisciplinary teams and
supervised by a multidisciplinary team of instructors, the students surveyed
the neighborhood, conducted interviews with the residents, and observed
in the schools; they identified the community's strengths, challenges, and
needs, and then completed a literature review. Each team then came up with
a plan, which they presented to the city officials in a public forum. The "win-
ning" team had its proposal accepted by the community representatives, and
work commenced to bring the plan to fruition. The cross-disciplinary collaboration and the dialogue across disciplines—sometimes contentious—
led to a deeper, multifaceted understanding of the issues faced by the community. The team of instructors, each representing one of the disciplines
represented by the students, offered some lectures but primarily served as
coaches and facilitators of the students' efforts. The teams developed plans
and recommendations that were rich, complex, and many-layered. Most of
all, the motivation level, energy, and interest of the student teams remained
high throughout the duration of the project.

Structured Problem Solving.   Structured problem solving is an activity that can be used in conjunction with several other cooperative learning approaches. The instructor assigns students to groups in a way that
maximizes diversity and comes up with a relevant problem, preferably one
that has its foundations in practice, at least in educational settings. Each

group member is assigned a number by the instructor. Group me[mbers] discuss their task and prepare themselves for each member to res[pond] dependently of other group members. The instructor calls on indiv[iduals] from each group to respond, making sure that numbers are used to cal[l] students randomly. Calling on students in this way forces each member t[o] take the task seriously and to be accountable for outcomes. It is important to know that this technique might be frightening for students who do not speak up in class. Therefore, it should be used advisedly and in a nonthreatening way, perhaps by starting off with a simple question where there is no danger of being wrong. It could also be a technique that the instructor uses later rather than earlier during the term, when students have settled into the class and its routines.

Send-a-Problem.   The Send-a-Problem technique can be used as a way to get groups to discuss and review material or find potential solutions to problems related to content information. Students should come to class having read a (preferably) difficult or complex piece related to course topics. In class, each member of a group generates a problem or a question related to the reading, writes it down on a card, and then seeks responses from the other members of the group. If the group can come up with a consensus, the answer is written on the back of the card; if not, modifications are made. The appropriate sides of the cards are marked with a Q(uestion) and an A(nswer). Each group sends its pack of cards to another group, and the process is repeated. If the second group agrees with the first group's answers, they proceed to the next question; if not, they write their answer on the back of the card. Stacks of cards can thus be passed through several groups; when the stack is finally returned to the first group, it has the collective wisdom of the class represented in the card stacks.

A variation on the Send-a-Problem technique would be to get groups to discuss a real-world problem for which there may not be one correct answer. The same process as before is followed, with the first group brainstorming solutions to a problem that is written on the outside of a folder. Solutions are listed on pieces of paper and placed in the folder. The folder is passed to the next group, which takes three to five minutes to brainstorm solutions and then repeats the process, without viewing the other groups' solutions. The final group to get the folder examines all the solutions, collaboratively prioritizes them, and then presents the folder to the original group.

Jigsaw Groups.   First developed by Elliot Aronson in the early 1970s (Aronson and Patnoe 1997), jigsaw groups are a type of cooperative learning approach that works well in the higher education classroom, particularly when the material to be studied is complex, lengthy, and multifaceted. It can also be used effectively to build motivation in students, to form learning groups, and to ensure that all students are accountable not only for their own learning but for that of the group.

A jigsaw group usually consists of five or six members who are selected by the instructor on the basis of diversity in age, experience, knowledge, gender, and ethnicity. The day's reading is broken down by the instructor into five or six different, stand-alone sections and a leader is appointed. Each group member independently reads his or her section twice. Then the instructor forms temporary "expert groups" that include one representative from each group (students who have read the same section of the passage). "Expert group" members take some time to share their understanding of the material with one another. They may collaboratively engage in critical reflection and self-correction, add to their knowledge base, have difficult concepts explained, and develop three or four group learnings that they can take back to their original groups. Each member returns to his or her original group and teaches the material to the rest of the group. The instructor then assigns a quiz or a short exam to test student learning. There are more complex variations of the jigsaw classroom, which have enjoyed varying degrees of success.

Service Learning Projects.   Based in the literature on experiential learning (Kolb 1984) and a relative newcomer to college campuses, service learning is an authentic learning experience that allows students to provide meaningful service to communities, critically reflect on their experiences, frame them within the context of ongoing social issues, and work with peers and community members to strengthen those communities. Team-based service learning projects require students to collaboratively engage in critical reflection on social issues. For example, student teams could research and then serve the homeless populations in their hometowns and then present their findings in class. Service learning is becoming increasingly popular as students discover the potential of an activity that combines volunteerism with college credit.

Critical Incidents and Simulations.   The use of mini-scenarios that are typically found in a discipline (e.g., a teaching incident in education courses) could be used to promote collaborative critical reflective thinking. These incidents have been used in education courses (Chittooran 2014; Griffin 2003) and tend to be successful typically because there is realism and an emotional component to the incidents that appeal to students who may be used to lecture material.

Simulations usually involve complex, structured situations that simulate real-world problems and require students to role-play to come up with a solution. Most simulations ask students, working individually or in teams, to play the role of opposing stakeholders in a problematic situation or an unfolding drama. Taking on the values and acting the part of a stakeholder usually gets students emotionally invested in the situation. The key aspect of simulations, though, is that of perspective taking, both during the simulation exercise and afterward. Following the simulation, there is usually a lengthy discussion where students reflect on the simulation and explore their own actions and those of others. This is where important concepts and lessons emerge. Simulations may be difficult for Asian students, who may not be used to the vulnerability that such experiences demand of them.

One way around this that the author has found useful with international students with limited English proficiency is to allow the more confident students to take on active speaking roles; other students can be assigned to nonspeaking roles such as observers or recorders of information. In this way, all students can be fully invested in the simulation.

Think-Pair-Share and Variations.   Think-pair-share is touted as an approach that may be particularly suited to instructors and students who are new to collaborative learning, in that the investment of effort and time is minimal and the risks are low. It begins with the instructor providing a discussion prompt based on a reading or key point from a lecture. Students reflect on the reading independently and then discuss their ideas with a partner. One advantage of this approach is that everyone is involved, and knowledge construction begins when students share what they know and don't know with their peers. Students then offer comments to be shared with the whole group, and because they have had a chance to think about and get feedback on the issue in the safety of a small group, the ensuing discussion tends to be richer and more complex. For a variation, the instructor may avoid using whole-group discussion; instead, students are asked to write down their thoughts on note cards and submit them to the instructor, who then reads selected comments out loud to the class. This variation may be particularly helpful with shy students who can say anonymously what they really feel, for those who are unaccustomed to speaking up in class (as many Asian students might be), or if the topic is a controversial one (e.g., abortion).

Guided Reciprocal Peer Questioning.   Guided reciprocal peer questioning can be an excellent activity to generate discussion among student groups about a specific topic. First, the instructor lectures briefly about a particular topic, followed by a short reading or writing assignment. The instructor then gives the students a set of broad question stems, such as: "What is the main idea of . . . ?" "How does this relate to what I've learned before?" "What conclusions can I draw about . . . ?" Students work independently to create their own questions based on the material they have just read, without necessarily having to answer their own questions. The purpose is to get them to think about content they have read, not just in a superficial way, but in a way that requires reflection. Once they are grouped into learning teams, the students can offer up each question for discussion and response.

Roundtable.   A roundtable discussion can be an excellent way to introduce students to brainstorming. It may be particularly useful when the questions posed have no right answers ("Do you support the death penalty and why?"), or when the problem is a complex multilayered one. It can also be useful in learning groups where previous instruction has focused on discovering "the one right answer," as is often the case in traditional Asian classrooms. As with all brainstorming, the key is flexibility in thinking and willingness to entertain all possibilities; this may be difficult for some Asian

NEW DIRECTIONS FOR TEACHING AND LEARNING • DOI: 10.1002/tl

students, who may have been taught that there is one right answer for every question.

First, the instructor assigns students to groups, introduces or reviews the rules of brainstorming, and presents students with a problem for solution. Students write their solutions on cards and then go around the small group, taking turns reading their responses out loud. The critical aspect of this phase of the roundtable is respectful listening to and lack of judgment on others' responses, however unworkable or unrealistic they seem. At the end, when everyone has had a turn, the group can critically reflect on each solution and come up with a consensus. Alternatively, the instructor can gather all responses anonymously, and then either choose to share all the responses with the rest of the class, or simply engage the class in a whole-group discussion based on selected points.

Focused Listing.   The technique of focused listing requires students, working individually, to generate words to define or describe important concepts, and can be good practice for brainstorming. Once students have completed this activity, instructors can use these lists to facilitate group and class discussion. For example, students in a course on teaching middle school mathematics may be asked to list five to seven phrases that describe what a motivated middle school student might do in the classroom. From there, the instructor might ask students to get together in small groups to discuss the lists, or to select the points on which they can all agree. This technique can be combined with a number of other collaborative learning techniques (e.g., roundtable) to build a powerful learning structure in the classroom.

One-Minute Papers.   The use of one-minute papers can be a very effective, if simple, way of facilitating critical reflection on course processes and gathering feedback about how the class is going and if and how the instructor needs to make changes. Usually completed in an impromptu fashion at the end of a class period, one-minute papers can ask students to answer the following questions in writing, preferably anonymously: What important or useful thing did you learn today? What was unclear to you today? What do you want to know more about?

The answers can be gathered and read out loud to the class. They can also be shared within small groups and then with the larger class so that students can come up a consensus, if wished. One-minute papers require students to critically reflect on what they have learned that day and may be useful for students who are reluctant to speak up or ask questions in class or for those from cultural backgrounds (as in Asia) where questioning one's teachers would be considered inappropriate and disrespectful. These papers can be used by faculty and students as a check on instructional effectiveness, to get information quickly about student comprehension, and, finally, to plan instruction.

The preceding section has described a variety of learning activities that use reading and writing to enhance critical reflection. All students in the higher education classroom can benefit from these techniques because they involve students, make the classroom a community of learning, and encourage shared responsibility for the learning process as well as its outcomes.

Conclusion

This chapter has offered a number of ways to use reading and writing activities to enhance critical reflection and thus to contribute to collaborative knowledge construction in the college classroom. While this collaborative approach to learning admittedly represents a marked shift in the way many instructors in Asian classrooms teach their students and the way many students in Asian settings are used to learning, it is believed that it offers promise for improved learning among students. This collaborative approach requires a significant change in how both instructors and students approach the teaching and learning process. However, given these tools for enhanced learning, as well as a willingness to embrace their challenges, Asian students should be armed to contribute to their own learning, and to compete effectively in the global arena.

References

Aronson, E., and S. Patnoe. 1997. *The Jigsaw Classroom: Building Cooperation in the Classroom*, 2nd ed. New York: Longman.

Barrows, H. S. 1996. "Problem-Based Learning in Medicine and Beyond: A Brief Overview." In *Bringing Problem-Based Learning to Higher Education: Theory and Practice*, edited by L. Wilkerson and W. H. Gijselaers, 3–12. San Francisco: Jossey-Bass.

Brookfield, S. 1995. *Becoming a Critically Reflective Teacher*. San Francisco: Jossey-Bass.

Chittooran, M. M. 2014. *Analyzing a Neighborhood Dilemma: Implications for Critical Reflection and Collaborative Learning*. Unpublished paper, Saint Louis University.

Dewey, J. 1933. *How We Think: A Restatement of the Relation of Reflective Thinking to the Educative Process*. New York: Heath & Co.

Driscoll, M. P. 2009. *Psychology of Instruction for Learning*, 4th ed. Boston: Allyn & Bacon.

Griffin, M. L. 2003. "Using Critical Incidents to Promote and Assess Reflective Thinking in Pre-Service Teachers." *Reflective Practice* 4:207–220.

Guo, T. 2015. "Learning the Confucian Way." In *From the Confucian Way to Collaborative Knowledge Co-Construction*, New Directions for Teaching and Learning, no. 142, edited by G. J. van Schalkwyk and R. C. D'Amato, 5–18. San Francisco: Jossey-Bass.

Gustafson, K. L., and J. W. Bennett. 2002. *Promoting Learner Reflection: Issues and Difficulties Emerging from a Three-Year Study*. Ft. Belvoir, GA: Defense Technical Information Center.

Hatton, N., and D. Smith. 1995. "Reflection in Teacher Education: Towards Definition and Implementation." *Teaching and Teaching Education* 11:33–49.

Kaplan, D. S., W. H. Rupley, S. Sparks, and A. Holcomb. 2007. "Comparing Traditional Journal Writing with Journal Writing Shared over E-Mail List Serves as Tools for Facilitating Reflective Thinking: A Study of Preservice Teachers." *Journal of Literacy Research* 39:357–387.

Kolb, D. 1984. *Experiential Learning: Experience as the Source of Learning and Development*. Englewood Cliffs, NJ: Prentice-Hall.

Lyman, F. 1981. "The Responsive Classroom Discussion." In *Mainstreaming Digest*, edited by A. S. Anderson, 109–113. College Park, MD: University of Maryland College of Education.

Mayer, R. E. 2008. *Learning and Instruction*, 2nd ed. Upper Saddle River, NJ: Pearson.

Mezirow, J. 1990. "How Critical Reflection Triggers Transformative Learning." In *Fostering Critical Reflection in Adulthood*, edited by J. Mezirow, 1–20. San Francisco: Jossey-Bass.

Mezirow, J. 1998. "On Critical Reflection." *Adult Education Quarterly* 48:185–198.

Ormrod, J. E. 2011. *Human Learning*, 6th ed. Upper Saddle River, NJ: Pearson.

Ormrod, J. E. 2013. *Educational Psychology: Developing Learners*, 8th ed. Boston: Pearson.

Qian, G., and J. Pan. 2002. "A Comparison of Epistemological Beliefs and Learning from Science Text between American and Chinese High School Students." In *Personal Epistemology: The Psychology of Beliefs about Knowledge and Knowing*, edited by B. K. Hofer and P. R. Pintrich, 365–385. Mahwah, NJ: Lawrence Erlbaum Associates.

Schommer-Aikins, M., and M. Easter. 2008. "Epistemological Beliefs' Contributions to Study Strategies of Asian Americans and European Americans." *Journal of Educational Psychology* 100:920–929.

Shadiow, L. K. 2013. *What Our Stories Teach Us: A Guide to Critical Reflection for College Faculty*. San Francisco: Jossey-Bass.

Short, P. M., and J. S. Rinehart. 1991, October. "Critical Reflective Thinking as a Means of Professional Development." *ERIC Papers*. Paper presented at the Annual Meeting of the University Council for Educational Administration, Baltimore, Maryland.

Tsay, M., and M. Brady. 2010. "A Case Study of Cooperative Learning and Communication Pedagogy: Does Working in Teams Make a Difference?" *Journal of the Scholarship of Teaching and Learning* 10:78–89.

University of Texas Center for Teaching and Learning. n.d. "Engagement." http://ctl.utexas.edu.

van Schalkwyk, G. J. 2015. "Outcomes-Based Collaborative Teaching and Learning in Asian Higher Education." In *From the Confucian Way to Collaborative Knowledge Co-Construction*, New Directions for Teaching and Learning, no. 142, edited by G. J. van Schalkwyk and R. C. D'Amato, 19–40. San Francisco: Jossey-Bass.

Woolfolk, A. 2013. *Educational Psychology: Active Learning Edition*, 12th ed. Boston: Pearson Education.

Xu, Y., J. A. M. Farver, Z. Zhang, Q. Zeng, L. Yu, and B. Cai. 2005. "Mainland Chinese Parenting Styles and Parent-Child Interaction." *International Journal of Behavioral Development* 29:524–531.

Yong, S., Y. S. Park, B. S. K. Kim, J. Chiang, and C. M. Ju. 2010. "Acculturation, Enculturation, Parental Adherence to Asian Cultural Values, Parenting Styles, and Family Conflict among Asian American College Students." *Asian American Journal of Psychology* 1:67–69.

MARY M. CHITTOORAN *is a school psychologist on the faculty of the Department of Education at Saint Louis University, St. Louis, Missouri.*

INDEX

develop capacities to make meaning in, and of, the world. This volume will be of interest to educators across the disciplines and in diverse roles.
ISBN 978-11190-63384

TL140   ***Inclusive Teaching: Presence in the Classroom***
Cornell Thomas, Editor
Faculty today are faced with a much more diverse student body each year, and this challenge must be met in the classroom by caring faculty who trust that all students can learn and bring different aspects of their lives to the learning environment. In this volume of *New Directions for Teaching and Learning*, the authors focus on the importance of inclusive teaching and the role faculty can play in helping students achieve by adjusting their approach to teaching by believing that each student has the ability to learn, though not necessarily in the same way. To teach with a focus on inclusion means to believe that every person has the ability to learn. It means that most individuals want to learn, to improve their ability to better understand the world in which they live, and to be able to navigate their pathways of life. This volume includes the following topics:
• best practices for teaching students with social, economic, gender, or ethnic differences
• adjustments to the teaching and learning process to focus on inclusion
• strategies for planning and teaching that help learners connect what they already know with the information presented
• environments that maximize learners' academic and social growth
The premise of inclusive teaching works to demonstrate that all people can and do learn. Educators and administrators can incorporate the techniques of inclusive learning and help learners retain more information.
ISBN 978-11190-36470

TL139   ***Multidisciplinary Collaboration: Research and Relationships***
Karen Weller Swanson, Editor
The Scholarship of Teaching and Learning (SoTL) has been a movement in higher education for many years. This volume of *New Directions for Teaching and Learning* focuses on this scholarship and how collaborations among and between disciplines can strengthen education and the ways in which students are taught. The community of scholars that exists at any institution can provide a fertile ground for interdisciplinary collaboration that can enliven the educational process and the research that supports it. The chapters within this volume are written by individuals from many different disciplines who teach and who use SoTL to inform their own practice and as a method to share what they have done with others.
ISBN 978-11189-80569

TL138   ***Hidden Roads: Nonnative English-Speaking International Professors in the Classroom***
Katherine Grace Hendrix, Aparna Hebbani, Editors
This issue uses the powerful narrative of autoethnography to make visible the existence of international professors and teaching assistants who speak English as a Second Language. These important, but often invisible, individuals contribute daily to the education of students within the US postsecondary educational system. Much of the research on international

faculty in the classroom has focused on gathering voices of US students as the subjects, so there is a notable absence in the literature of voices of the nonnative English speaker in the classroom. This volume adds to the literature by covering a variety of experiences, such as faculty of color teaching intercultural communication, international teaching assistants' attitudes toward their US students, and the challenges to existing cultural assumptions in the US classroom. These experiences—in the form of challenges and contributions—are foregrounded and highlighted in their own right.
ISBN 978-11189-23092

TL137 ***Active Learning Spaces***
Paul Baepler, D. Christopher Brooks, J. D. Walker, Editors
When we think about some of the main concepts that are embodied in the recent teaching and learning paradigm shift, we think about student engagement, active learning, collaboration, and peer instruction. And when we reflect upon the impediments to making these things happen in courses, instructors often indict the physical spaces in which they teach. The configuration of classrooms, the technology within them, and the behaviors they encourage are frequently represented as a barrier to enacting student—centered teaching methods, because traditionally designed rooms typically lack flexibility in seating arrangement, are configured to privilege a speaker at the front of the room, and lack technology to facilitate student collaboration. But many colleges and universities are redesigning the spaces in which students learn, collapsing traditional lecture halls and labs to create new, hybrid spaces—large technology-enriched studios—with the flexibility to support active and collaborative learning in larger class sizes. With this change, our classrooms are coming to embody the 21st-century pedagogy which many educators accept, and research and teaching practice are beginning to help us to understand the educational implications of thoughtfully engineered classrooms—in particular, that space and how we use it affects what, how, and how much students learn.
ISBN 978-11188-70112

TL136 ***Doing the Scholarship of Teaching and Learning: Measuring Systematic Changes to Teaching and Improvements in Learning***
Regan A. R. Gurung, Janie H. Wilson, Editors
The Scholarship of Teaching and Learning (SoTL) should be an integral part of every academic's life, representing not only the pinnacle of effortful teaching, but also standing side by side with more conventional disciplinary scholarship. Although practiced by many instructors for years, SoTL has garnered national attention resulting in a spate of new journals to publish pedagogical research. SoTL helps students, fosters faculty development, and has been integrated into higher education in *Scholarship of Teaching and Learning Reconsidered* (Hutchings, Huber, & Ciccone, 2011). This volume provides readers with challenges that will motivate them to engage in SoTL and take their pedagogical research further. We include many key features aimed to help both the teacher new to research and SoTL and also researchers who may have a long list of scholarly publications in non-pedagogical areas and who have not conducted research.
ISBN 978-11188-38679

NEW DIRECTIONS FOR TEACHING AND LEARNING
ORDER FORM SUBSCRIPTION AND SINGLE ISSUES

DISCOUNTED BACK ISSUES:

Use this form to receive 20% off all back issues of *New Directions for Teaching and Learning.*
All single issues priced at **$23.20** (normally $29.00)

TITLE	ISSUE NO.	ISBN

*Call 1-800-835-6770 or see mailing instructions below. When calling, mention the promotional code JBNND
to receive your discount. For a complete list of issues, please visit www.josseybass.com/go/ndtl*

SUBSCRIPTIONS: (1 YEAR, 4 ISSUES)

☐ New Order   ☐ Renewal

U.S.	☐ Individual: $89	☐ Institutional: $335
CANADA/MEXICO	☐ Individual: $89	☐ Institutional: $375
ALL OTHERS	☐ Individual: $113	☐ Institutional: $409

*Call 1-800-835-6770 or see mailing and pricing instructions below.
Online subscriptions are available at www.onlinelibrary.wiley.com*

ORDER TOTALS:

Issue / Subscription Amount: $ _____

Shipping Amount: $ _____
(for single issues only – subscription prices include shipping)

Total Amount: $ _____

SHIPPING CHARGES:

First Item $6.00
Each Add'l Item $2.00

*(No sales tax for U.S. subscriptions. Canadian residents, add GST for subscription orders. Individual rate subscriptions must
be paid by personal check or credit card. Individual rate subscriptions may not be resold as library copies.)*

BILLING & SHIPPING INFORMATION:

☐ **PAYMENT ENCLOSED:** *(U.S. check or money order only. All payments must be in U.S. dollars.)*

☐ **CREDIT CARD:**   ☐ VISA   ☐ MC   ☐ AMEX

Card number _____ Exp. Date _____

Card Holder Name _____ Card Issue # _____

Signature _____ Day Phone _____

☐ **BILL ME:** *(U.S. institutional orders only. Purchase order required.)*

Purchase order # _____
Federal Tax ID 13559302 • GST 89102-8052

Name _____

Address _____

Phone _____ E-mail _____

Copy or detach page and send to: **John Wiley & Sons, One Montgomery Street, Suite 1000,
San Francisco, CA 94104-4594**

Order Form can also be faxed to: **888-481-2665**

PROMO JBNND

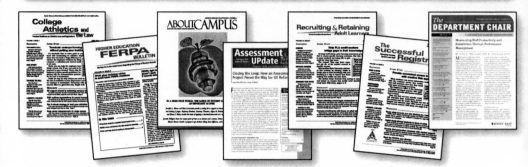